THE COUNTRY MUSIC QUIZ BOOK

THE COUNTRY MUSIC QUIZ BOOK

Don and Barbara
Humphreys

DOLPHIN BOOKS
Doubleday & Company, Inc.
Garden City, New York
1978

Library of Congress Cataloging in Publication Data

Humphreys, Don.
  The country music quiz book.

  1. Country music—Miscellanea. I. Humphreys,
Barbara, joint author. II. Title.
ML63.H92   784
ISBN: 0-385-12397-3
Library of Congress Catalog Card Number 77–76274

CONTENTS

QUIZZES

QUIZZES

SITTIN' IN THE BALCONY—FIRST REEL

Country music and Hollywood had crossed paths way before Robert Altman's popular film *Nashville*. Many country artists have been associated with Hollywood's finest and not so fine productions. See if you can identify the personality and his or her film.

1. _____ sang the title song in *North to Alaska* and _____ _____ _____.

2. Folksy balladeer won an Academy Award as Best Supporting Actor for his performance in _____ _____ _____.

3. *The Chartreuse Caboose* was the title of a movie starring a female singer from California named _____ _____.

4. _____ _____ was featured in such movie classics as *Duel in the Sun* and *Wilson,* but he is best remembered for his many pictures with Gene Autry.

5. _____ _____ portrayed Mary Magdalene in her husband's film of the Christ story entitled _____ _____.

6. The gold record _____ _____ _____ _____, written and recorded by Bobbie Gentry, became a movie with the same title.

7. _____ _____ did the singing while actor George Hamilton did the acting in _____ _____ _____. Later, however, with Connie Francis in *A Time to Sing and a Time to Cry* he did both.

8. *Platinum High School, Sex Kittens Go to College,* and *College Confidential* were three of the films that featured _____ _____.

9. Super picker _____ _____ had distinguished himself as an actor in two Burt Reynolds pictures, _____ _____ _____ _____ _____ and _____.

10. The film _____ was billed as the first psychedelic western and featured, among others, the Cajun fiddler _____ _____.

(*Answers page 115*)

STEP UP TO THE BAR

The ten tunes below are drinking songs. How many can you match with the singer of the song?

1. "Day Drinking"
2. "Blues Plus Booze"
3. "Don't Come Home A-Drinkin' "
4. "Jim, Jack and Rose"
5. "Whiskey, Whiskey"
6. "Tiny Bubbles"
7. "Drinkin' My Baby (Off My Mind)"
8. "Bottles and Barstools"
9. "I'm Gonna Tie One on Tonight"
10. "Swinging Doors"

A. Wilburn Brothers
B. Jerry Lee Lewis
C. Merle Haggard
D. Eddie Rabbitt
E. Johnny Bush
F. Tom T. Hall, Dave Dudley
G. Loretta Lynn
H. Stonewall Jackson
I. Rex Allen
J. Nat Stuckey

(*Answers page 115*)

SCRAMBLER #1

Scrambled below are the names of four of country music's most popular performers. One clue to help untangle them: they all made the unbelievable jump from a life behind bars to a place in the spotlight.

1. LDACNDOIEALVA
2. DFRENYDREDEF
3. GAERDAMGHRLE
4. NORUNIJEDZHOYGR

(*Answers page 115*)

12

HOW THEY GOT THERE

Match the following lines with the songs that they belong to.

1. "thumbed a diesel down"
2. "raced my horse with a Spaniard's pole"
3. "I rode a freight train north"
4. "Ridin' in the brand-new wagon"
5. "I was walking down the street"
6. "pole the pirogue down the bayou"
7. "I went tripping through the snow"
8. "driving that new Cadillac"
9. "we marched back to town in our dirty ragged pants"
10. "Well, our golden jet is airborne"

A. "Detroit City"
B. "The Battle of New Orleans"
C. "Me and Bobby McGee"
D. "Ode to Little Brown Shack Out Back"
E. "May the Bird of Paradise Fly Up Your Nose"
F. "Welfare Cadillac"
G. "When the Wagon Was New"
H. "Bloody Mary Morning"
I. "Jambalaya"
J. "Tennessee Stud"

(*Answers page 116*)

PURE GOLD

Below are the titles of fifteen albums that earned the coveted gold record, indicative of a million sales. Can you name the artist who recorded the album?

1. *Ring of Fire* _____
2. *My World* _____
3. *Distant Drums* _____
4. *For the Good Times* _____
5. *The Fighting Side of Me* _____
6. *Easy Loving* _____
7. *The Silver Tongued Devil and I* _____
8. *The Happiest Girl in the Whole USA* _____
9. *Hello Darlin'* _____
10. *The Country Way* _____
11. *Rose Garden* _____
12. *Honey* _____
13. *Harper Valley PTA* _____
14. *Take Me Home, Country Roads* _____
15. *Baby Don't Get Hooked on Me* _____

(Answers page 116)

EVERYBODY TALKS ABOUT

The weather plays an important part in the titles of many country songs. Listed below are ten such songs. Your job is to fill in the missing weather condition that completes the title.

1. "Baby, It's _____ Outside"
2. "A Living _____"
3. "Catch a Little _____"
4. "Gentle _____ of Home"
5. "_____ _____ and Gold Sand"
6. "Honey, Toast and _____"
7. "When the _____ Is on the Roses"
8. "Soft _____"
9. "Big _____"
10. "_____ in My Heart"

(Answers page 117)

DEAR JOHN CRISSCROSS

This crisscross utilizes just a few of the seemingly endless songs with the name John in the title. Each answer helps you complete another, hence the crisscross. The clues below give the titles of the song. You are to provide the last names of the artist or artists who recorded the song.

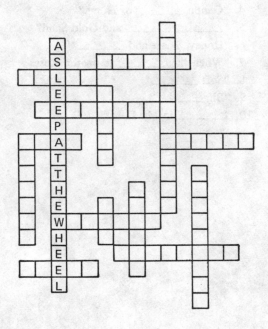

3 letters:
  "Johnny One Time"

4 letters:
  "Big Bad John"

5 letters:
  "Mr. and Mrs. John Smith"
  "Johnny B. Goode" (*not* Chuck Berry)
  "John Wesley Hardin"

6 letters:
  "John Henry, Jr."
  "Johnny Reb"
  "Hey There Johnny"

7 letters:
  "Johnny's Cash and Charlie's Pride"
  "Johnny Lose It All"

8 letters:
  "Dear John"

9 letters:
  "A Dear John Letter"
  "Johnny My Love"

12 letters:
  "Forgive Me, John"

16 letters:
  "The Letter That Johnny Walker Read"

(*Answers page 117*)

THE TROUBADOURS

A remarkable number of country recording stars from Jimmie Rodgers to the present have been prolific and gifted songwriters. The following quiz focuses on a number of the modern singer-songwriters and their songs. In column one are listed two songs from the pen of the same songwriter. Listed in column two, out of order, are the authors. In column three, also out of order, is a third tune penned by the star. Your task is to match the writer and the third song with the two tunes in column one.

1. "Homecoming," "One Hundred Children"   A. Roger Miller   a. "Padre"

2. "I Walk the Line," "Folsom Prison Blues"   B. Dolly Parton   b. "Coal Miner's Daughter"

3. "England Swings," "Dang Me"   C. Willie Nelson   c. "Loving Her Was Easier"

4. "Together Again," "My Heart Skips a Beat"   D. Marty Robbins   d. "We Used To"

5. "White Line Fever," "I Can't Be Myself"   E. Loretta Lynn   e. "Crying Time"

6. "For the Good Times," "The Pilgrim"   F. Johnny Cash   f. "Branded Man"

7. "You Ain't Woman Enough," "I Know Him"   G. Merle Haggard   g. "Faster Horses"

8. "Hello Walls," "Touch Me"   H. Tom T. Hall   h. "Kansas City Star"

9. "You Gave Me a   I. Buck Owens   i. "Flesh and Blood"
   Mountain," "My
   Woman, My
   Woman, My
   Wife"

10. "Coat of Many   J. Kris Kristofferson   j. "Funny How Time
    Colors," "In the   Slips Away"
    Good Old Days"

(*Answers page 118*)

LEADER OF THE BAND—FIRST SET

Your task in this quiz is to match the singers in column one with the
names of their bands listed in column two.

1. Merle Haggard   A. Po' Boys
2. Roy Acuff   B. Southern Gentlemen
3. Johnny Cash   C. Party Times
4. Dave Dudley   D. Sweet Thangs
5. Kinky Friedman   E. Strangers
6. Ernest Tubb   F. Blue Boys
7. Tom T. Hall   G. Smokey Mountain Boys
8. Jim Reeves   H. Tennessee Three
9. Sonny James   I. Texas Jew Boys
10. Hank Thompson   J. Brazos Valley Boys
11. Mel Tillis   K. Roadrunners
12. Wanda Jackson   L. Troubadours
13. Jimmy Buffett   M. Statesiders
14. Bill Anderson   N. Coral Reefers
15. Nat Stuckey   O. Storytellers

(*Answers page 118*)

THE MEMORY LINGERS ON

Country lyrics are truly some of the most memorable ever written. See if you can name the song titles which contain these famous opening lines.

1. "Don't look so sad, I know it's over"
2. "I tried so hard, my dear, to show"
3. "You think you know the smile on his lips"
4. "If heartaches brought fame in love's crazy game"
5. "You were mine for just a while, now you're puttin' on the style"
6. "As I look at the letters that you wrote to me"
7. "Memories that linger in my heart"
8. "If you loved me half as much as I love you"
9. "My yellow rose of Texas packed up and left this mornin'"
10. "When I'm lonely I think of someone"

(Answers page 119)

STABLEMATES

We all know that Roy Rogers' trusty steed was Trigger, but do you remember the name of Dale Evans' horse? Here are five clues to help you find the names of five famous horses. The circled letters, when assembled correctly, will form the name of a sixth equine wonder.

1. Trigger's stablemate   (＿)＿ ＿ ＿ ＿ ＿ ＿ ＿ ＿ ＿
2. Smiley Burnette's horse   ＿ ＿ ＿ ＿ ＿(＿)＿
3. He belonged to Gene   ＿ ＿ ＿(＿)＿ ＿(＿)＿
4. Rex Allen rode him   ＿ ＿ ＿(＿)
5. Tex Ritter's faithful   ＿ ＿ ＿(＿)＿   ＿ ＿ ＿ ＿ ＿

6. (＿)(＿)(＿)(＿)(＿)(＿)   Stuart Hamblen's horse

(Answers page 119)

ODD ONE OUT

One name from each of the following groups was not born in the same state as the other two. Cast the odd one out.

1. TENNESSEE
   (a) Carl Smith (b) Connie Smith (c) Melba Montgomery
2. ARKANSAS
   (a) Don Bowman (b) Elton Britt (c) Jim Ed Brown
3. CALIFORNIA
   (a) Sammi Smith (b) Cliffie Stone (c) Wynn Stewart
4. OKLAHOMA
   (a) Bonnie Owens (b) Buck Owens (c) Merle Kilgore
5. KENTUCKY
   (a) Loretta Lynn (b) Stringbean (c) Red Steagall
6. MISSOURI
   (a) Porter Wagoner (b) Leroy Van Dyke (c) Dolly Parton
7. FLORIDA
   (a) Slim Whitman (b) Johnny Dollar (c) Gram Parsons
8. LOUISIANA
   (a) Floyd Cramer (b) Jerry Lee Lewis (c) Carl Belew
9. TEXAS
   (a) Webb Pierce (b) Claude Gray (c) Bob Wills
10. MISSISSIPPI
    (a) Tammy Wynette (b) Johnny Paycheck (c) Elvis Presley
11. ALABAMA
    (a) Hank Williams (b) Freddie Hart (c) Johnny Duncan
12. ILLINOIS
    (a) Billy Grammer (b) Tex Williams (c) Jean Shepard
13. WISCONSIN
    (a) Danny Davis (b) Dave Dudley (c) Pee Wee King
14. OHIO
    (a) Buell Kazee (b) Roy Rogers (c) Bobby Bare
15. ARIZONA
    (a) Rex Allen (b) Jody Miller (c) Norma Jean

(*Answers page 120*)

RADIO BARN DANCES

The famous radio barn dance shows featuring country music became an important factor in the music's spreading popularity. Listed below are ten of the most famous early shows. Opposite them and out of order are the cities from where the shows originated. How many can you match?

1. WBAP Barn Dance	A.	Shreveport
2. Renfro Valley Barn Dance	B.	Dallas
3. WWVA Jamboree	C.	Knoxville
4. National Barn Dance	D.	Wheeling
5. Ozark Jubilee	E.	Fort Worth
6. Boone County Jamboree	F.	Chicago
7. Tennessee Barn Dance	G.	Richmond
8. Lone Star Barn Dance	H.	Springfield
9. Louisiana Hayride	I.	Cincinnati
10. Old Dominion Barn Dance	J.	Renfro

(*Answers page 120*)

SCRAMBLER #2

The letters scrambled below spell the names of four of Nashville's premier sessionmen.

1. SEASEVSCTANMLR
2. LSOROPADOBTNH
3. RORCLYAFEMD
4. ELCACMIHCYOR

(*Answers page 121*)

GOING IN CIRCLES—PART ONE

This puzzle progresses in spiral fashion. The last word in the first title is the first word in the second title and so on. There are thirteen songs all together. If that doesn't scare you off completely, you'll notice the middle title is filled in so that you will know if you're on the right track or not. If you're not, you might want to glance at the list of singers who've recorded these songs. Maybe it'll help. Maybe.

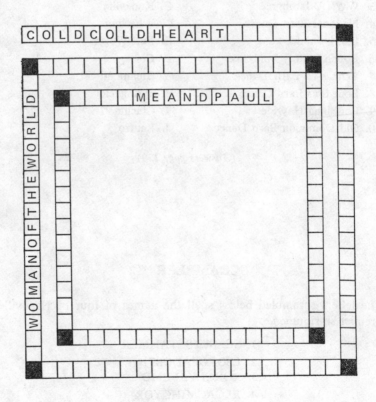

Hank Williams
Bob Wills and Tommy Duncan
Jerry Reed
Bobby Bare
Elvis Presley
Loretta Lynn
Tom T. Hall

Mills Brothers
Johnny Cash
Lefty Frizzell
Eddy Arnold
Lynn Anderson
Willie Nelson

(*Answers page 121*)

YOU CAN'T, I CAN'T

Complete the title of each of the following "can't" songs. The name of the artist is provided to help you out.

1. "You Can't _____ _____"   Billy Mize
2. "I Can't _____"   Connie Smith
3. "You Can't _____ _____ _____.   Ernie Ashworth
   _____ _____"
4. "I Can't _____ _____ _____"   Don Gibson
5. "You Can't _____ _____ _____"   Cal Smith
6. "I Can't _____ _____"   Merle Haggard
7. "You Can't _____ _____ _____ &   Statler Brothers
   _____ _____"
8. "I Can't _____ _____ _____   George Jones
   _____"
9. "You Can't _____ _____ _____"   Carl Smith
10. "I Can't _____ _____ _____   Wilburn Brothers
    _____"

(*Answers page 122*)

WITH PEN IN HAND

Column one lists the hit song, column two lists the singer who had the hit. Can you supply the third column listing the writer or writers of the song?

1. "Honey" Bobby Goldsboro _____
2. "Behind Closed Doors" Charlie Rich _____
3. "A Boy Named Sue" Johnny Cash _____
4. "Harper Valley PTA" Jeannie C. Riley _____
5. "Detroit City" Bobby Bare _____
6. "Gentle on My Mind" Glen Campbell _____
7. "You Don't Know Me" Eddy Arnold _____
8. "Please Help Me, I'm Falling" Hank Locklin _____
9. "Delta Dawn" Tanya Tucker _____
10. "Tennessee Waltz" Patti Page _____
11. "Blue Eyes Crying in the Rain" Willie Nelson _____
12. "Heartaches by the Number" Ray Price _____
13. "The Son of Hickory Holler's Tramp" Johnny Darrell _____
14. "Green Green Grass of Home" Porter Wagoner _____
15. "Have I Told You Lately That I Love You" Kitty Wells and Red Foley _____

(*Answers page 122*)

OUTLAWS

A group of performers whose music and/or life styles have not matched the expectations of the more conservative elements of country music have been branded as outlaws. How many black sheep can you identify?

1. His Fourth of July celebration is famous from coast to coast. _____

2. He claims to have killed a man on Death Row. _____

3. This artist wrote the often-recorded "Willie the Wandering Gypsy and Me." _____

4. She is married to none other than Waylon Jennings. _____

5. This outlaw was the leader of a brother act judged the most outstanding country group of the past decade. _____

6. He wrote the classic "Mr. Bojangles." _____

7. One of the few women in the group, she won a gold record with her recording of a Kris Kristofferson tune. _____

8. He won a Grammy for his version of "MacArthur Park." _____

9. He was the leader of one of the most popular rock quintets in the late sixties. _____

10. Some would say he started the whole outlaw cult with his original approach to country music. _____

(*Answers page 123*)

I'M A TRUCK

Trucking songs have never been as popular as they are today. Perhaps the truck has the same appeal to a new generation as the railroad had to an older one. However, the truck song is not an entirely new phenomenon. Here are ten songs and a selection of artists. Select the correct artists.

1. "I'm a Truck"
   (A) Hank Thompson (B) Red Simpson (C) Buck Owens
   (D) Warner Mack
2. "White Line Fever"
   (A) Merle Haggard (B) Hoyt Axton (C) Tom T. Hall
   (D) Sonny James
3. "A Tombstone Every Mile"
   (A) Bobby G. Rice (B) Bobby Helms (C) Michael Murphey
   (D) Dick Curless
4. "Diesel on My Tail"
   (A) Red Steagall (B) Johnny Sea (C) Jim & Jesse (D) The
   Dillards
5. "Convoy"
   (A) Don Bowman (B) Archie Campbell (C) John Hartford
   (D) C. W. McCall
6. "Six Days on the Road"
   (A) Porter Wagoner (B) Dave Dudley (C) Jerry Lee Lewis
   (D) Conway Twitty
7. "Giddyup Go"
   (A) Minnie Pearl (B) Charlie Daniels (C) Red Sovine
   (D) Tommy Cash
8. "I'm a Trucker"
   (A) Johnny Russell (B) Johnny Bush (C) Johnny Rodriguez
   (D) Johnny Dollar
9. "Truck Drivers Blues"
   (A) Dick Feller (B) Stoney Edwards (C) Moon Mullican
   (D) Dock Boggs

10. "Roll On, Big Mama"
    (A) Kenny Stone   (B) Ronnie Milsap   (C) Troy Seals   (D) Joe
    Stampley

(*Answers page 123*)

SHOOTIN' STARS

Many country singers in the thirties and forties were brought to Hollywood to star in westerns exploiting the enormous popularity of country and western music. How many of the western movie makers listed below can you match with the clues provided?

1. Smiley Burnette was his sidekick.   a. Roy Rogers
2. Recorded a number of hits with   b. Gene Autry
   Margaret Whiting.
3. Penned and recorded the hit "Deck of   c. Jimmy Wakely
   Cards."
4. Later starred on TV in *Frontier Doctor*.   d. Stuart Hamblen
5. Hall of Famer featured in New York   e. Rex Allen
   production of *Green Grow the Lilacs*.
6. He left the Sons of the Pioneers for a   f. Tex Ritter
   movie career.
7. Shared writing credit and recorded, "I   g. Bill Boyd
   Dreamed of Hillbilly Heaven."
8. The King of Western Swing   h. Eddie Dean
9. Author of "This Old House"   i. T. Texas Tyler
10. "The Cowboy Rambler"   j. Bob Wills

(*Answers page 123*)

NAME THAT STAR—PART ONE

This is a Hide and Hunt. We hide 'em, you hunt 'em. In this diagram are the last names of forty great male figures in country music. The names run forward and backward, up, down, and diagonally in all directions, but always in a straight line. We've given you some clues below. Remember, last names only.

```
J I M E S T O N J A C K S O N Z I S E V
C E L M O L H D E A N G H E N E E R G U
L C N Y V F L E N B U K C T T E F F U B
A R A N O P R A I D C T L E N E L L A R
R E C R I E R Y H S R U R T S A Y R L A
K F D O G N P E G A S C T Y T U E I A K
A F W N O I G U H T A E E T C U L L N C
F U L L U R L S O N J O L E N R D M O O
N B D H A M I L T O N I V R V R U I S D
O T C O C H R A N N C G G H U A D S E D
T S E T S U H A G G A R D S N C D D S A
R A N T S F A L Y E M O K A K O O Y I R
O B D E A T O N E L P Y A C C A S P V C
H O M R K B R N K F B M Y Z G A W B A I
P A O I A C M Y S F E E T G A L E Y I S
J D N L N O I H U A L L A N C R A S H G
G S E W R Y N D H O L H E T U Z L S A S
L Y O F R E T T F P M J N A F I Z G E A
A R B F R I Z Z E L L E P H F E L V A R
B N O S R E D N A M D E I R F L I T T S
```

1. A _ _ _ _ _, Roy
2. A _ _ _ _, Buddy
3. A _ _ _ _ _, Rex
4. A _ _ _ _ _ _, Eddy
5. A _ _ _ _ _ _ _ _, Bill

6. A _ _ _ _ _, Chet
7. A _ _ _ _, Gene
8. B _ _ _, Bobby
9. B _ _ _ _, Jim Ed
10. B _ _ _ _ _ _, Jimmy
11. C _ _ _ _ _ _ _ _, Archie
12. C _ _ _ _ _ _, Henson
13. C _ _ _, Johnny
14. C _ _ _ _, Roy
15. C _ _ _ _ _ _, Hank
16. C _ _ _ _, Cowboy
17. C _ _ _ _ _ _ _, Crash
18. C _ _ _ _ _ _, Dick
19. D _ _ _, Jimmy
20. D _ _ _ _ _ _, Jimmy
21. D _ _ _ _ _, Roy
22. D _ _ _ _ _, Dave
23. F _ _ _ _, Red
24. F _ _ _ _, Lester
25. F _ _ _, Tennessee Ernie
26. F _ _ _ _ _ _ _ _, Kinky
27. F _ _ _ _ _ _ _ _, Lefty
28. G _ _ _ _ _, Tompall
29. H _ _ _ _ _ _ _, Merle
30. H _ _ _, Tom T.
31. H _ _ _ _ _ _ _ _ _ _, George
32. H _ _ _, Freddie
33. H _ _ _ _ _, Johnny
34. H _ _ _ _ _, Ferlin
35. I _ _ _, Burl
36. J _ _ _ _ _ _, Stonewall
37. J _ _ _ _, Sonny
38. J _ _ _ _ _ _ _, Waylon

(*Answers page 124*)

OCCUPATION SONGS

Country music has always been a paean to the working man in all his diversity. In this quiz, ten of those songs have been listed in column one, omitting the occupation from the title. You are to choose the occupation from the scrambled list in column two. Column three is a scrambled list of the people who recorded the song. You are to match their names with the completed song title.

1. "The Cute Little _____"	A. Newsboy	a. Johnny Russell
2. "I'm a _____"	B. Salesman	b. Hank Thompson
3. "The Cajun _____"	C. D.J.	c. Stonewall Jackson
4. "If I Were a _____"	D. Hairdresser	d. Stoney Edwards
5. Greenwich Village Folksong _____"	E. Stripper	e. Rusty & Doug
6. "Jimmy Brown the _____"	F. Waitress	f. Jim Ed Brown
7. "B.J. the _____"	G. Sailor	g. Kitty Wells
8. "Only Me and My _____"	H. Sheriff	h. Johnny Cash & June Carter
9. "Whoa, _____"	I. Trucker	i. Mac Wiseman
10. "Hey, _____"	J. Carpenter	j. Jim & Jesse

(*Answers page 124*)

HOW'S THIS FOR OPENERS?—PART ONE

Listed below are the opening lines from fifteen classic country tunes. How many of the songs can you identify from their opening lines?

1. "I am weak, but Thou art strong"
2. "Now blue ain't the word for the way I feel"
3. "Ten years ago on a cold dark night"
4. "Put your sweet lips a little closer to the phone"
5. "Busted flat in Baton Rouge, headin' for the trains"
6. "My bills are due, and baby needs shoes"
7. "Deep within my heart lies a melody"
8. "The corn was dry, the weeds were high when Daddy took to drinkin'"
9. "What a beautiful thought I am thinking"
10. "Goodbye, Joe, me gotta go, me-oh, my-oh"
11. "Well, at birth my Mom and Papa called a little boy Ned"
12. "Come listen, you fellers, so young and so fine"
13. "It was the third of June, another sleepy, dusty Delta day"
14. "The other night, dear, as I lay sleeping"
15. "When you live in the country, everybody is your neighbor"

(*Answers page 125*)

THE EYES OF TEXAS ARE UPON YOU

Just as Texas natives seem to dominate country music, an unusually high number of songs are about the Lone Star State. Fill in the blank words in the following titles.

1. "_____ _____ Texas _____" Roy Drusky
2. "_____ _____ _____ Texas" Ernest Tubb
3. "_____ Texas _____" George Hamilton IV
4. "Texas _____" Guy Clark
5. "_____ _____ Texas" Jimmie Rodgers
6. "Texas _____" Stuart Hamblen
7. "_____ Texas" W. Lee O'Daniel
8. "Texas _____" Harry McClintock
9. "Texas _____" B. W. Stevenson
10. "Texas _____" David Allan Coe

(*Answers page 125*)

CHRISTMAS

In the quiz below are five Christmas songs recorded by three country greats. See if you can fill in the titles of the songs. We've given you some help to start you off.

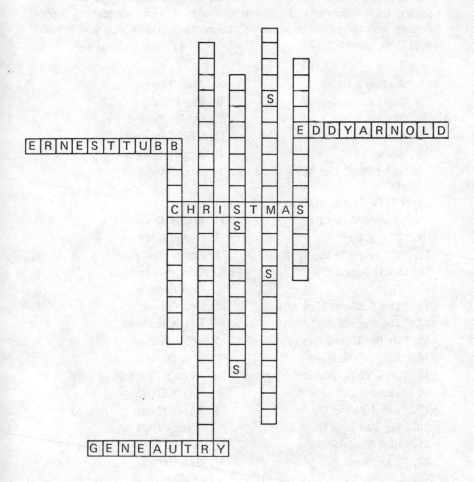

(*Answers page 126*)

DOUBLE WHAMMIES

It is not uncommon for country hits to become simultaneously a pop-rock hit, or for the pop-rock hit to simultaneously hit the country charts. (Elvis Presley records do it repeatedly.) Listed below are twenty-five records that have been hits in both fields—for the same singer. Listed opposite them, out of order, are the singers of these double whammies. How many of the cross-over hits can you match with their hit-makers?

1. "Be Bop a Lula"	A. Anne Murray
2. "My Elusive Dreams"	B. Ray Price
3. "Waterloo"	C. Donna Fargo
4. "Hello Walls"	D. Glen Campbell
5. "Snowbird"	E. Johnny Horton
6. "Baby Don't Get Hooked on Me"	F. Gene Vincent
7. "Oh Lonesome Me"	G. Eagles
8. "Harper Valley PTA"	H. Jimmy Dean
9. "Danny Boy"	I. Duane Eddy
10. "We'll Sing in the Sunshine"	J. Ferlin Husky
11. "Splish Splash"	K. Stonewall Jackson
12. "Gone"	L. Carl Perkins
13. "The Battle of New Orleans"	M. Don Gibson
14. "The Race Is On"	N. Everly Brothers
15. "By the Time I Get to Phoenix"	O. Bobby Vinton
16. "King of the Road"	P. Mac Davis
17. "Let's Think About Living"	Q. Jeannie C. Riley
18. "Three Bells"	R. Bobby Darin
19. "Rebel Rouser"	S. Roger Miller
20. "Big Bad John"	T. Freddy Hart
21. "Blue Suede Shoes"	U. Jim Ed Brown
22. "Lyin' Eyes"	V. Gail Garnett

23. "The Happiest Girl in the   W. Bob Luman
    Whole USA"
24. "Easy Loving"   X. Faron Young
25. "Bye Bye Love"   Y. George Jones

(*Answers page 127*)

BEER DRINKING MUSIC

In this matching quiz, every song title either has beer in the title or refers to the brew. Your task is to match the beer song with the singer of the song.

 1. "Pop a Top"   A. Tom T. Hall
 2. "A Six Pack to Go"   B. Ben Colder
 3. "What Made Milwaukee   C. Johnny Russell
    Famous"
 4. "Beer Drinkin' Honky Tonkin'   D. Jim Ed Brown
    Blues"
 5. "15 Beers Ago"   E. Hank Thompson
 6. "Beer Drinking Music"   F. Johnny Sea
 7. "Red Necks, White Socks, and   G. Jerry Lee Lewis
    Blue Ribbon Beer"
 8. "I Like Beer"   H. Billy Mize
 9. "Lone Star Beer and Bob Wills' I. Ray Sanders
    Music"
10. "Three Six Packs"   J. Red Steagall

(*Answers page 127*)

PARDON ME, MISS

Each of the following artists recorded a hit tune featuring a girl's name in the title. Can you pick the correct name of each star's hit?

1. Bobby Helms
   a. Marilyn   b. Wanda   c. Jacqueline

2. Merle Haggard
   a. Barbara   b. Joyce   c. Carolyn

3. Johnny Cash
   a. Kathy   b. Kate   c. Laverne

4. Tommy Overstreet
   a. Gwen   b. Lynn   c. Bonnie

5. Stonewall Jackson
   a. Melinda   b. Leona   c. Patricia

6. Billy Grammer
   a. Becky   b. Liza   c. Mabel

7. Eddy Arnold
   a. Molly   b. Sharon   c. Sherry

8. Moon Mullican
   a. Jaynie   b. Mona Lisa   c. Mary Lou

9. Porter Wagoner
   a. Julie   b. Lou Ann   c. Dollie

10. J. Ryles
    a. Veronica   b. Kay   c. Nadine

11. Tanya Tucker
    a. Bonnie Lou   b. Loretta   c. Dawn

12. Sonny James
    a. Fay   b. Annie   c. Jenny Lou

13. Jim Reeves
    a. Anna Marie   b. Carol Ann   c. Tracey

14. Bobby Lewis
    a. Mary Lou   b. Brenda   c. Mona

15. Doyle Holly
    a. Sue Ann   b. Lila   c. Becky

(*Answers page 128*)

THE STATE OF THINGS

Below are listed twelve songs with a state in the title. Only the state's name has been left out. Your task is to fill in the blank with the correct state to complete the title.

1. "Blue Moon of _____"
2. "Way Out West in _____"
3. "My Little Home in _____"
4. "The _____ Hills"
5. "_____ Woman"
6. "_____ Man"
7. "Northeast _____ Mississippi County Bootlegger"
8. "Wicked _____"
9. "Saginaw, _____"
10. "_____ Sunshine"
11. "North to _____"
12. "_____ Wild Man"

(Answers page 128)

PIONEERS

The following quiz tests your knowledge of the early pioneers of country music. Simply match the proper name with the clue provided.

1. Generally acknowledged as the first country artist to be recorded for commercial purposes.

   A. Ralph Peer

2. The Hall of Fame family known for their close harmonies and religious tunes.

   B. Jimmie Rodgers

3. Responsible for recording many of the early pioneer performers. He formed OKEH records before moving to RCA.

   C. Dock Boggs

4. The first solo singing star of country music came from Texas. His real name was Marion Slaughter, but he chose the names of two West Texas towns to serve as his stage name.

   D. Fiddlin' John Carson

5. One of the great pioneer songwriters and entertainers in country music.

   E. Riley Puckett

6. He was the singing star of the Grand Ole Opry before Roy Acuff, and a most talented five-string banjoist.

   F. The Carter Family

7. Country music's first superstar: The Blue Yodeler.

   G. Bradley Kinkaid

8. Blind singer-guitarist with the popular string band called the Skillet Lickers; he later became one of the most successful solo record artists of the twenties and thirties.

   H. Carson Robison

9. Known as "The Kentucky Mountain Boy," he sang the traditional ballads of the hills and became one of the most recorded talents of the twenties.

   I. Vernon Dalhart

10. He was a hard-working coal miner who became a legend with his unique banjo style.

    J. Uncle Dave Macon

(Answers page 128)

GOING IN CIRCLES—PART TWO

This is another spiral puzzle. That is, the last word in the first title is the first word in the second title and so on. There are twelve song titles in this puzzle. The recording artists are listed below to give you some help as well as the first, sixth, and last titles. Good luck. You'll need it.

Loretta Lynn	Johnny Cash	Ernie Ashworth
Dottie West	Hank Thompson	Ferlin Husky
Dallas Frazier	Johnny Dallas	Hank Locklin
Wynn Stewart	Elvis Presley	Barbara Mandrell

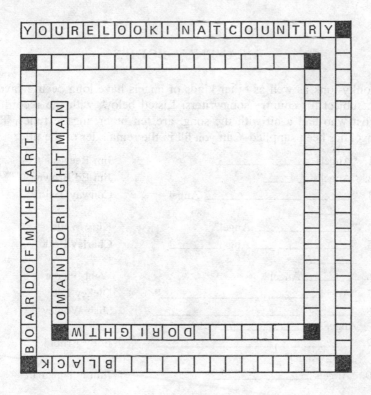

(*Answers page 129*)

SCRAMBLER #3

The four following scrambled names were all gold record winners in the year 1971.

1. CARRPYIE
2. MISTASMHIM
3. NELDSARYONNN
4. DERTADFERIH

(*Answers page 129*)

HEAVENLY BODIES

Honky-tonk as well as other kinds of angels have long been a favorite subject for country songwriters. Listed below, with the recording artist who had a hit with the song, are ten other angelic tunes. The angel has been supplied. Can you fill in the remainder of the title?

1. "Angels _____ _____"   Jim Reeves
2. "Angel's _____"   Jim Ed Brown
3. "_____ _____ _____ Angel
      _____"   Conway Twitty
4. "_____ _____ Angel"   Kitty Wells
5. "_____ _____ Angel _____
      _____"   Charley Pride
6. "_____ Angel"   Webb Pierce
7. "Angels, _____ _____ _____"   Dickey Lee
8. "_____ _____ _____ _____
      Angel's _____ _____"   Sheb Wooley
9. "_____ _____ _____ _____
      _____ Angel"   Eddy Arnold
10. "Angels _____ _____"   Jimmy Newman

(*Answers page 130*)

42

POLITICS AND PATRIOTS

This quiz asks you to remember many of the political and patriotic moments in country music.

1. Name the tune recorded by Jimmy Dean telling of the brave exploits of John F. Kennedy.
2. The ultra-conservative "Day of Decision," warning of the grave dangers facing America, was made popular by whom?
3. "Stars and Stripes on Iwo Jima" clearly showed the sacrifice necessary for freedom. Name the recording artist on this World War II song.
4. One of the most popular of the political singers was Woody Guthrie. One of his well-known ballads used the name of a character from Steinbeck's *Grapes of Wrath*.
5. The partisan feelings of Billy Cox in this song praising FDR's re-election are obvious.
6. One of the Opry's wittiest commentators in song described the hard facts of life in such songs as "All I've Got's Gone."
7. This recitation praising America and originally made popular by a Canadian broadcaster was one of Tex Ritter's last recordings.
8. The textile mill protest song, "Weave Room Blues," was recorded by what popular act?
9. Although she had only one commercial recording ("Kentucky Miner's Wife"), this singer-songwriter was a spokesman through her songs both to and for the coal miners of Kentucky.
10. Merle Haggard stirred liberals in the sixties with his "Okie from Muskogee," but his following hit was even more polarizing.

(*Answers page 130*)

HOMESICK HIDE AND HUNT

This is a Hide and Hunt. We hide 'em. You hunt 'em. In the diagram below are the last names of fifteen songwriters who have written songs of home and reminiscence. The names run forward and backward, up, down, and on the diagonal in all directions, but always in a straight line. We've provided some clues. Remember, last names only.

```
A L L E Z Z I R F U G M A H I
K U O S R D G S S R E P O T N
M A L K V I N E L B M A H A L
G E R N I L O N T R P O P N Y
S R E G D O R O M A R D O Y N
L L V A H U S J R T O N I R N
J A N S O V K T O G I V R O N
S N E L T I O N R I S L N B O
O L D N E N O S I B O R L I H
L O U D E R M I L K B P I I L
T L S V I C T B U R U N Y S S
K A H G O G D E T T E R L U D
I S A S H A V O M A T V K N I
L O L U N E V A K U N I L A R
Y A L L V U N P A I P G A H O
```

1. "Alabama"—Ira and Charlie _____
2. "Carry Me Back to the Mountains"—Carson _____
3. "Coal Miner's Daughter"—Loretta _____
4. "Daddy and Home"—Elsie McWilliams and Jimmie _____
5. "Detroit City"—Danny Dill, Mel _____
6. "8 More Miles to Louisville"—Grandpa _____
7. "Green Green Grass of Home"—Curley _____
8. "Homecoming"—Tom T. _____
9. "In the Good Old Days (When Times Were Bad)"—Dolly _____

10. "Mocking Bird Hill"—Vaughn _____
11. "Mom and Dad's Waltz"—Lefty _____
12. "Take Me Home, Country Roads"—Bill and Taffy Danoff, John _____
13. "That Silver-Haired Daddy of Mine"—Jimmy Long, Gene _____
14. "This Ole House"—Stuart _____
15. "Tobacco Road"—John D. _____

(*Answers page 131*)

A THING ABOUT TRAINS

More than one country performer has confessed a "thing" about trains in song. How many can you match with their recorded train songs?

1. "City of New Orleans"   A. Roy Acuff
2. "Mystery Train"   B. Hank Snow
3. "Freight Train Blues"   C. Roger Miller
4. "Movin' On"   D. Vernon Dalhart
5. "Waiting for a Train"   E. Jimmie Rodgers
6. "Orange Blossom Special"   F. Elvis Presley
7. "Wabash Cannon Ball"   G. Johnny Cash
8. "Night Train to Memphis"   H. Red Foley
9. "Engine, Engine #9"   I. Steve Goodman
10. "The Wreck of the Old 97"   J. A. P. Carter

(*Answers page 131*)

PRIME TIME

Syndicated television carries countless country shows to large audiences every week, but the leap to prime time television on one of the three major networks in anything more than a spot as a guest artist is rare. The quiz below asks you to remember some of those who have made it.

1. It all started for _____ _____ with his summer replacement for the Smothers Brothers.

2. _____ _____ won an Emmy for one of his shows in a series of specials.

3. _____ _____ got the call from Andy Williams to be his summer replacement show's host.

4. A card and letter campaign revived _____ _____'s weekly variety show after the network had canceled it.

5. In the dramatic TV series "The Bold Ones," _____ _____ played the senior member of a crusading team of attorneys.

6. Before gaining his own weekly variety show, _____ _____ _____ made TV history portraying Lucy's country cousin.

7. With Fess Parker, _____ _____ starred in the TV series of "Mr. Smith Goes to Washington."

8. NBC tried _____ _____ twice, hosting a weekly variety hour, once in a tuxedo and once with his shirt open.

9. The half-hour variety show given _____ _____ strait-jacketed his multiple and unpredictable talents.

10. _____ _____ gained national popularity as a regular on the Lawrence Welk Show.

(*Answers page 132*)

WE MAKE BEAUTIFUL MUSIC TOGETHER

In column one are the titles of some country duets. In columns two and three are the names of the singers who recorded these songs together. Pair the singers, then match them with the songs they teamed up on.

1. "After the Fire Is Gone"
2. "Under Your Spell Again"
3. "Someday We'll Be Together"
4. "Rings of Gold"
5. "Yes, Mr. Peters"
6. "We Must Have Been Out of Our Minds"
7. "Loose Talk"
8. "Removing the Shadow"
9. "After Closing Time"
10. "Bushel and a Peck"

A. Roy Drusky
B. Don Gibson
C. Jimmy Wakely
D. Conway Twitty
E. David Houston
F. Hank Williams, Jr.
G. Waylon Jennings
H. Buck Owens
I. George Jones
J. Bill Anderson

a. Melba Montgomery
b. Jan Howard
c. Dottie West
d. Priscilla Mitchell
e. Lois Johnson
f. Loretta Lynn
g. Barbara Mandrell
h. Margaret Whiting
i. Rose Maddox
j. Jessi Colter

(Answers page 132)

ALL OF ME

There are seven song titles needed to complete this puzzle. All the titles have something in common. To help you get started, the last names of all the recording artists have been scattered at random throughout the puzzle.

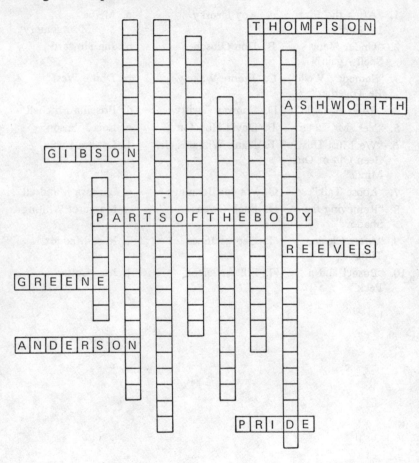

(*Answers page 133*)

WHAT'S IN A NAME?—PART ONE

Below are listed ten names—the real names of the ten country stars rather than their recording names. In the second column, you will find ten hit records. Your task is to match the hit record with the recording artist's real name.

1. Seth Ward	A.	"Nobody Wins"
2. Donald Lytle	B.	"Young Love"
3. Muriel Deason	C.	"Heartbreak U.S.A."
4. Otis Dewey	D.	"Deck of Cards"
5. Wynette Pugh	E.	"Big Bad John"
6. Harold Jenkins	F.	"The Bridge Washed Out"
7. Brenda Mae Tarpley	G.	"The Lovin' Machine"
8. James Loden	H.	"More than Yesterday"
9. David Luke Myrick	I.	"Hello Darlin'"
10. Warner MacPherson	J.	"D-I-V-O-R-C-E"

(*Answers page 134*)

COWBOYS

With the introduction of western influence into country music, the cowboy has become as much a part of country music as the guitar. Saddle up for another straight answer quiz about the cowboy in country music.

1. Everyone called this popular recording artist "Cowboy." You will remember him for his recordings of "Filipino Baby" and "Alabam."

2. Marty Robbins' song of a different kind of cowboy in different clothing in this cowboy tune.

3. This popular performer bills himself as "The Mysterious Rhinestone Cowboy."

4. Ed Bruce made the hit charts with this song warning mothers about cowboys.

5. He introduced many hobo and cowboy songs to America. Among them is "The Cowboy's Prayer."

6. Bobby Bare made the charts with this song telling how divorce often separates fathers and sons.

7. Michael Murphey created a cult following with this modern-day cowboy song.

8. The Grammy Award-nominated "Rhinestone Cowboy" was a big hit for what country star?

9. The principals in the title of this Patsy Sledd hit were the same as those in the title of a Gary Cooper–Merle Oberon movie.

10. Jonathan Edwards jumped high onto the country charts with his recording of this cowboy song written by Darrell Statler.

(*Answers page 134*)

INDIANS

The following is a straight answer quiz. There is no room for guesses, just straight answers about an important part of country music—the American Indian.

1. Hank Williams' favorite wooden Indian.
2. Loretta Lynn used a twist on Indian words to good advantage in the title of this hit song.
3. Johnny Cash recorded an entire album dedicated to the American Indian and his travails. Name the album.
4. Being part-Indian was part of the attraction and billing of this popular star's rise in country music, beginning with his hit "Gonna Find Me a Bluebird."
5. This pop hit about a certain Indian was later turned into a country hit by Sonny James.
6. The Cherokee Cowboys combined two of the elements of western mythology and formed the name for what star's band?
7. Another Indian artist and his group have scored a hit in country music with such recordings as "Pledging My Love." Name them.
8. "Don't Go Near the Indians" was a hit in both pop and country music for this popular recording star.
9. Michael Murphey has written and recorded several songs dealing with American Indians, past and present. Best known, however, is his song about a great Apache chief. Name the song.
10. Name the country star who had a million seller on the classic "Indian Love Call."

(*Answers page 135*)

COUNTRY IMPORTS

If you fill in the correct answers below, you will have the names of five country acts born outside the United States. Then take the circled letters and unscramble them to find the Country Music Hall of Famer whose origins are other than the U.S.A.

1. This duo started in folk music but eventually had a successful syndicated country television show.
   __ __ __ and (__) __ (__) __ __ __
2. A Canadian, this vocalist has often appeared with Glen Campbell.
   (__) __ __ (__) __ __ (__) __ __ (__)
3. This red-haired singer is often called Miss Country Soul.
   __ __ __ __ __ (__) (__) __ __ __
4. This superstar is a favorite with pop audiences as well as country fans.
   __ __ __ __ __ __ __ (__) __ (__) __ __-__ __ __ __
5. This old-timer is known for his splendid wardrobe.
   (__) (__) __ __ __ __ __ __
6. (__) (__) (__) (__) (__) (__) (__) (__) (__) (__) (__) (__)

(*Answers page 135*)

WAY BACK WHEN

The road to success is rarely a straightaway. Often the detours can be as varied and as interesting as the success itself.

1. Before becoming one of Nashville's super songwriters, he was a Rhodes Scholar.

2. The leader of one of country music's most raucous new groups was an accomplished artist and sculptor.

3. He came from the farm lands of Arkansas, but before he reached the country spotlight, he worked selling vacuum cleaners.

4. A former guitar maker, he is now the shaper of such songs as "Desperados Waiting for a Train."

5. He was a Ph.D. candidate and welfare worker before his first album, *Got No Bread, No Milk, But We Sure Got a Lot of Love,* hit the record stalls.

6. Being a featured cartoonist for *Playboy* magazine is not a common background for a composer, but the author of "Queen of the Silver Dollar" and other hits has just that in his past.

7. He lost fingers working at the sawmills before his songs were discovered by Bobby Bare, Kris Kristofferson, and Waylon Jennings.

8. A mortuary assistantship was in the past of this superstar.

9. She learned hairdressing and worked in a beauty shop before she garnered country music's award as top female vocalist.

10. As a schoolteacher, he wrote songs to help his students learn American history. Millions learned a little history from his composition "The Battle of New Orleans."

(*Answers page 136*)

MARY, MARY

The following ten hit tunes all have "Mary" in the title. Can you fill in the rest of the title? The recording artist has been provided as an additional clue.

1. "_____ Mary"   Billy Walker
2. "Mary Ann _____"   Burl Ives
3. "Mary's _____"   Claude King
4. "_____ _____ Mary"   Tompall & Glaser Brothers
5. "_____ Mary _____"   Country Gentlemen
6. "_____ _____ _____
   _____ Mary"   Everly Brothers
7. "Mary _____ _____
   _____"   Stonewall Jackson
8. "Mary _____ _____"   Bobby Helms
9. "Mary's _____ _____"   Carl Belew
10. "_____ Mary Lou"   Bobby Lewis

(Answers page 136)

TAKE ME OUT TO THE BALL GAME

For some unknown reason, there is a strong baseball background in the lives of several country music stars. This straight answer quiz explores the backgrounds.

1. A sunstroke prevented this Country Music Hall of Famer from continuing his tryout for the Yankees and turned him back to music.
2. He played with the L. A. Angels and even went to spring training with Casey Stengel's marvelous Mets, but he ended up breaking new ground in country music rather than baseball.
3. Through country music he rose from a night clerk to millionaire to owner of the California Angels.
4. He was a good minor league pitcher until an injury sidelined him. As a country singer, he became the truckers' favorite.
5. He was moving up in the St. Louis Cardinals organization as a pitcher, but, instead of following in the steps of Dizzy Dean, he became the "Country Gentleman" of country music.
6. Another good ballplayer who also wrote and recorded a few hundred songs sponsored the 1975 Music City Softball Champions.
7. He was a good hitting pitcher in Florida before he made a million seller out of "Rose Marie."
8. He went from pitcher in the Philadelphia Phillies' organization to overnight rock 'n' roll sensation to country stardom and duets with Loretta Lynn.
9. The Cleveland Indians lost this second-base prospect to Columbia Records and the millions of record buyers of such tunes as "Another" and "Anymore."
10. Another young pitcher with a promising baseball career before choosing country music, this man has combined music and acting, appearing in numerous TV shows and the movie *Stay Hungry*.

(*Answers page 137*)

NEW DAYS, NEW WAYS

One of the strongest elements inherent in the progressive country movement is its highly skilled number of songwriters bringing an exciting freshness to the country song. This quiz focuses on ten of those writers and a song of each of theirs that has attracted special attention. Your job is to match the song with its author.

1. Lee Clayton
2. Steve Young
3. Kinky Friedman
4. Guy Clark
5. Billy Joe Shaver
6. Michael Murphey
7. John Prine
8. Jessi Colter
9. Emmylou Harris
10. Mike Nesmith

A. "I'm Not Lisa"
B. "Desperados Waiting for the Train"
C. "Some of Shelley's Blues"
D. "Boulder to Birmingham"
E. "Sold American"
F. "Wildfire"
G. "Lonesome, On'ry and Mean"
H. "Paradise"
I. "Old Five and Dimers"
J. "Ladies Love Outlaws"

(*Answers page 137*)

SCRAMBLER #4

The scrambled letters below spell out the names of four of country music's brightest stars. In fact, they are all past winners of CMA's Entertainer of the Year.

1. YOCLKRAR
2. BLCLMGNPAEEN
3. NLTLNOATERY
4. HLRCREIHCIA

(*Answers page 137*)

PICK A PAIR—ONE

In this quiz, the title tells all. One of the answers in each group below does not go with the others. Give the letter of the misfit.

1. Singing partner of Anita Carter.
   (A) Waylon Jennings (B) Johnny Darrell (C) Buck Owens

2. Appeared in Burt Reynolds' movie, *W. W. and the Dixie Dancekings*.
   (A) Burl Ives (B) Don Williams (C) Jerry Reed

3. Gold Records for Kris Kristofferson.
   (A) "Why Me" (B) "Me and Bobby McGee" (C) "Jesus Was a Capricorn"

4. Recording partner with Red Foley.
   (A) Kitty Wells (B) Ernest Tubb (C) Loretta Lynn

5. They both made the hit charts singing "Cold, Cold Heart."
   (A) Jerry Lee Lewis (B) Hank Williams (C) Hank Williams, Jr.

6. Alex Harvey wrote two of them.
   (A) "Delta Dawn" (B) "Sweet Dream Woman" (C) "Reuben James"

7. Recording pseudonyms for Ferlin Husky.
   (A) Simon Crum (B) Terry Preston (C) Ben Colder

8. Recorded duets with Don Gibson.
   (A) Goldie Hill (B) Sue Thompson (C) Dottie West

9. Two more Texans.
   (A) Bob Luman (B) Merle Kilgore (C) Mickey Newbury

10. Both were put on suspension by the Grand Ole Opry.
    (A) Doug Kershaw (B) Hank Williams (C) Skeeter Davis

(Answers page 138)

NAME THAT STAR—PART TWO

In this puzzle are forty more great men in country music. Again, the names run forward and backward, up, down, and diagonally in all directions. We've given some clues below. Remember, last names only.

```
N E L P A Y C H E C K O W Y E K C U T S
G O N T I E O R N O M A E L S I R S M O
I T C E C R E I P E H L E O I L P I O Z
K R W A A H S T K S A W B C L G T H W E
I O L O M A N T R B I A J K L H A S E U
L N O S T A W E I S K C A L I Y O U N G
G O Y T E I K R C I T T W I T T Y B S I
O S L O S T E W A R T E N N J U D E E R
R L W U Z E U G S I R O D O R O O M A D
E T E Y M N U V I L S W R Y H U N O T O
S C N U K A C T V R L A S U E B S E W R
T R A V I S N R E L L I M R S L I S S U
H S W A N T I F C D N R W P E S S L E T
I R R N G B F P I W E O A I H P E E Y L
M E O I Y O U N R H G S S N L S P L R O
P G B T T U B B P O E R O P E L R U L P
B D B S H J L R I V E R K R M S I E T M
U O I W O R I N E L S O N D P O C A K I
T R N M O D A E J P E R K I N S H Y M L
K E S T E H R E N O G A W O N S K T O S
```

1. J_ _ _ _ _, George
2. K_ _ _ _ _ _ _, Doug
3. K_ _ _ _ _ _ _, Merle
4. K_ _ _ _, Pee Wee
5. K_ _ _ _ _ _ _ _ _ _ _ _ _ _, Kris
6. L_ _ _ _ _, Jerry Lee
7. L_ _ _ _ _ _ _, Hank

8. L_ _ _ _, Bob
9. M_ _ _ _, Dave
10. M_ _ _ _ _, Roger
11. M_ _ _ _ _, Bill
12. N_ _ _ _ _, Willie
13. O_ _ _ _, Buck
14. P_ _ _ _ _ _ _, Johnnie
15. P_ _ _ _ _ _, Carl
16. P_ _ _ _ _, Webb
17. P_ _ _ _ _ _, Elvis
18. P_ _ _ _, Ray
19. P_ _ _ _, Charlie
20. R_ _ _, Jerry
21. R_ _ _ _ _, Del
22. R_ _ _, Charlie
23. R_ _ _ _ _, Tex
24. R_ _ _ _ _ _, Marty
25. R_ _ _ _ _ _, Jimmie
26. R_ _ _ _ _ _ _ _, Johnny
27. R_ _ _ _ _ _, Johnny
28. S_ _ _ _, Carl
29. S_ _ _ _, Hank
30. S_ _ _ _ _ _, Wynn
31. S_ _ _ _ _ _, Nat
32. T_ _ _ _ _, Mel
33. T_ _ _ _ _ _ _, Hank
34. T_ _ _ _ _, Merle
35. T_ _ _, Ernest
36. T_ _ _ _, Conway
37. W_ _ _ _ _ _, Porter
38. W_ _ _ _ _, Doc
39. W_ _ _ _ _ _ _, Hank
40. W_ _ _ _, Bob
41. Y_ _ _ _, Faron

(*Answers page 138*)

AN AMUSING CRISSCROSS

This crisscross tests your knowledge of a part of country music that often doesn't involve a single note, yet is still part of the country heritage. We've provided clues for you. Answer them and try to find the appropriate place for the answer. Remember that they all intersect. We've started you off.

3 letters:
   Odie's partner
4 letters:
   Clements
   The Park Avenue Hillbilly (last name)
   Cousin _____
5 letters:
   Lonesome George
   There were four Oscars, but only one _____
   Part of a hit recording team
   Fibber's gal
6 letters:
   Part Two of that hit team in *5 letters*
   Campbell, and we don't mean soup
   She made it big in the movies (last name)
7 letters:
   Smiley
8 letters:
   Roy's sidekick
9 letters:
   "Chit Atkins" made him a star
   The Brasfields
10 letters:
   The late Opry and "Hee Haw" regular known by just one name
   A regular on "The Porter Wagoner Show"
11 letters:
   A newer comic seen on TV a lot
   Proprietors of the Jotem Down Store
   The grand lady of the Grand Ole Opry
12 letters:
   A big member of the "Hee Haw" cast
   "Hee Haw's" favorite relative
14 letters:
   Blackface minstrels at the Opry
16 letters:
   Better known as Amos and Andy

(*Answers page 139*)

DON'T

Complete the song titles below.

1. "Don't ＿＿＿＿ ＿＿＿＿ ＿＿＿＿   Joe South
   ＿＿＿＿ ＿＿＿＿ ＿＿＿＿"

2. "Don't ＿＿＿＿ ＿＿＿＿ ＿＿＿＿"   Carl Smith

3. "Don't ＿＿＿＿ ＿＿＿＿ ＿＿＿＿"   Buck Owens

4. "Don't ＿＿＿＿ ＿＿＿＿ ＿＿＿＿   Carl Butler
   ＿＿＿＿"

5. "Don't ＿＿＿＿ ＿＿＿＿ ＿＿＿＿   Norma Jean
   ＿＿＿＿ ＿＿＿＿"

6. "Don't ＿＿＿＿ ＿＿＿＿ ＿＿＿＿   Reno & Smiley
   ＿＿＿＿ ＿＿＿＿"

7. "Don't ＿＿＿＿ ＿＿＿＿ ＿＿＿＿   Ray Price
   ＿＿＿＿ ＿＿＿＿ ＿＿＿＿"

8. "Don't ＿＿＿＿ ＿＿＿＿ ＿＿＿＿   Don Gibson
   ＿＿＿＿"

9. "Don't ＿＿＿＿ ＿＿＿＿ ＿＿＿＿   Johnny Cash
   ＿＿＿＿ ＿＿＿＿"

10. "Don't ＿＿＿＿ ＿＿＿＿ ＿＿＿＿   Hank Thompson
   ＿＿＿＿ ＿＿＿＿"

(*Answers page 140*)

ROCK 'N' ROLL RETREADS

Old rock 'n' roll songs never die; they just become country hits. So many artists have been able to bring that certain magic to rock hits that turn them into pure country. Below in the first column are country and rock artists who have recorded the same song. Match them with the hit title they shared in the second column.

1. Buck Owens/Chuck Berry   A. "Dream Lover"
2. Bobby Lewis/Rick Nelson   B. "Promised Land"
3. Dickey Lee/Delaney & Bonnie   C. "Memphis"
4. Dr. Hook & the Medicine   D. "Show Me"
   Show/Sam Cooke
5. Jerry Lee Lewis/Big Bopper   E. "Endlessly"
6. Billy "Crash" Craddock/Bobby   F. "Raining in My Heart"
   Darin
7. Freddy Weller/Chuck Berry   G. "Chantilly Lace"
8. Barbara Mandrell/Joe Tex   H. "Only Sixteen"
9. Hank Williams, Jr./Slim Harpo   I. "Hello Mary Lou"
10. Sonny James/Brook Benton   J. "Never Ending Song of Love"

(Answers page 140)

MORE PIONEERS

In this quiz, you are to select the correct answers for the country music pioneer described.

1. A legendary fiddle player whose version of "Sally Goodin" is considered a classic.
   (A) Eck Robertson   (B) Levon Helm   (C) Ralph Peer

2. A pioneer recording artist on the Brunswick label with such records as "The Roving Cowboy" and "The Faded Coat of Blue." He was not only a singer and banjoist, but a Bible scholar and ordained minister.
   (A) Dock Boggs   (B) Buell Kazee   (C) Al Dexter

3. Patriarch of one of country music's most talented family clans.
   (A) Roy Acuff   (B) "Pop" Stoneman   (C) Whitey Ford

4. This blind Holiness preacher was one of country music's most prolific composers.
   (A) Buell Kazee   (B) Riley Puckett   (C) Andrew Jenkins

5. A popular songwriter in the twenties, he penned the patriotic "There's a Star Spangled Banner Waving Somewhere."
   (A) Red Sovine   (B) Red Foley   (C) Bob Miller

6. The decisive director of the Grand Ole Opry for many years.
   (A) Dave Macon   (B) John Lair   (C) George D. Hay

7. The leader of one of the twenties and thirties' most popular groups, the Skillet Lickers.
   (A) Gid Tanner   (B) Frank Walker   (C) Dorsey Dixon

8. A folk music authority, author of "Freight Train Blues," and leader of the Cumberland Ridge Runners.
   (A) Scotty Wiseman   (B) John Lair   (C) Carl Sprague

9. Leader of the Possum Hunters, the first old-time string band to be featured on WSM radio, the forerunner of the Opry.
   (A) George Hay   (B) Jimmy Thompson   (C) Humphrey Bate

10. Leader of North Carolina Ramblers whose first recording was the popular "Don't Let Your Deal Go Down."
    (A) Charlie Poole   (B) Clarence Ashley   (C) Henry Whittier

(*Answers page 140*)

WAR SONGS

The following quiz tests your memory of some of the war songs recorded over the years.

1. The Civil War was featured in a song entitled "The Battle of Bull Run." Name the singer of the saga song who recorded it.
2. Carl Smith recorded this pseudo-Revolutionary War song. Name the song.
3. This World War II tune, made popular by Red Foley, defiantly warned of what would happen when America met the enemy.
4. This song, popularized by Ernest Tubb during World War II, was recorded by Merle Haggard in the late sixties in response to Viet Nam. Name the song.
5. One of the most successful of all the war-oriented songs was Johnny Horton's recording of "The Battle of New Orleans." The author of the song said he wrote the tune to help teach students about the War of 1812. Name him.
6. The often-used theme of the death of a loved one was used by Jimmie Rodgers in this war tune written during World War I.
7. "Tell Them What We're Fighting For" was the declaration of this song popularized during the Viet Nam conflict. Name the singer of the song.
8. The angry World War II song "Cowards Over Pearl Harbor" was made popular by what Opry star?
9. Probably the most popular country war song ever recorded was written by Bob Miller and recorded by Elton Britt. Name the song.
10. One of the most strident of all the songs speaking out about Viet Nam was a blatant attack on the peace demonstrations by Stonewall Jackson. Name the song.

(*Answers page 141*)

NICKNAMES

A nickname confers almost an instant identity, a colorful addition to traditional country flair. In this quiz, you are asked to choose from the scrambled list of nicknames to show biz billings in the title associated with the star listed in column one.

1. Elvis Presley	A.	The Singing Fisherman
2. Bradley Kinkaid	B.	Cinderella Girl
3. Rex Allen	C.	Silver Fox
4. Stringbean	D.	Queen of the Yodelers
5. Jimmie Rodgers	E.	Mr. Sax
6. Connie Smith	F.	Crash
7. Billy Walker	G.	Solemn Old Judge
8. Rosalie Allen	H.	The Pelvis
9. Johnny Horton	I.	Round Mound of Sound
10. Charlie Rich	J.	Arizona Cowboy
11. Boots Randolph	K.	Traveling Texan
12. Bill Monroe	L.	Kentucky Wonder
13. Kenny Price	M.	Singing Brakeman
14. George D. Hay	N.	Father of Bluegrass
15. Billy Craddock	O.	Kentucky Boy with the Hound Dog Guitar

(*Answers page 141*)

YOURS AND MINE

Listed below are two columns of stars who had hits on the same song. In column three, you are to provide the song they shared.

1. Bobby Bare	Hank Snow	_____
2. Eddy Arnold	Slim Whitman	_____
3. Barbara Fairchild	Jean Shepard	_____
4. Pee Wee King	Hawkshaw Hawkins	_____
5. George & Gene	Rusty & Doug	_____
6. Waylon Jennings	Diana Trask	_____
7. Nat Stuckey	Carl Smith	_____
8. Skeeter Davis & Bobby Bare	Jean Shepard & Ferlin Husky	_____
9. Jack Greene	Kitty Wells	_____
10. Bill Justis	Ernie Freeman	_____
11. Cowboy Copas	Guy Mitchell	_____
12. Brenda Lee	Willie Nelson	_____
13. Hank Williams	Jerry Lee Lewis	_____
14. Red Foley	Ray Price	_____
15. Lynn Anderson	Osborne Bros.	_____

(*Answers page 142*)

THE DEVIL YOU SAY

If you fill in the correct answers below, you will have artists who recorded the following five "devil" songs. Then take the circled letters and unscramble them to form the name of the singer of a sixth recent "devil" song.

1. "Working Like the Devil for the Lord"
   __ __ (__) __ (__) __ __ __ __

2. "To Beat the Devil"
   (__) __ __ (__) __ __   __ __ __ __ (__) __ __ __

3. "Devil Woman"
   __ __ __ __ __   __ (__) __ __ __ __ (__) (__)

4. "Silver Tongued Devil and I"
   __ __ (__) __   __ __ __ __ __ __ __ __ __ __ __ __ (__)

5. "The Devil in Your Kisses (and the Angel in Your Eyes)"
   __ __ (__) __ __ __ (__) __ __

6.
   (__) (__) (__) (__) (__) (__)
   (__) (__) (__) (__) (__) (__)

(Answers page 142)

HARD TIME HUNGRYS

The down-and-out struggle to survive hard times has always been one of the touchstones of country music. In this quiz, you are asked to remember a few of those songs by filling in the blanks.

1. "If We Make It Through December" was a poignant and beautifully crafted song by _____ _____ expressing the struggle to overcome life's trying moments.

2. Johnny Cash and Ray Charles both made the Harlan Howard hardluck classic, _____, a hit.

3. Dolly Parton used a biblical framework in her song, _____ _____ _____ _____, to tell of childhood poverty.

4. O. C. Smith enjoyed pop music success with the country tune _____ _____ _____, which told of a poor woman's determination to feed and clothe her children.

5. John D. Loudermilk wrote the enormously successful _____ _____, which, like its Erskine Caldwell namesake, tells of life's poorer side.

6. Charlie Rich told of the yo-yo nature of life on his recording _____ _____ _____ _____ _____.

7. A concept album conceived by Shel Silverstein called *Hard Time Hungrys* was recorded by _____ _____.

8. Jimmy Buffett's _____ _____ _____ was a lighthearted look at life's rocky road.

9. Perhaps no one chronicled hard times better than did _____ _____ in his Dust Bowl ballads.

10. A comic approach to life's misfortunes was Carson Robison's classic _____ _____ _____ _____ _____.

(*Answers page 143*)

BALLADS OF . . .

Match the balladeer with his recorded ballad. Listed in column one are the singers and in the scrambled order in column two are the ballads.

1. Johnny Cash
2. Tennessee Ernie Ford
3. Tom T. Hall
4. Gordon Terry
5. Kinky Friedman
6. Flatt & Scruggs
7. Billy Grammer
8. Barry Sadler
9. Jim & Jesse
10. Roger Miller

A. "Ballad of John Dillinger"
B. "The Ballad of the Green Berets"
C. "Ballad of Thunder Road"
D. "Ballad of a Teenage Queen"
E. "Ballad of 40 Dollars"
F. "Ballad of J.C."
G. "Ballad of Jed Clampett"
H. "Ballad of Charles Whitman"
I. "Ballad of Davy Crockett"
J. "Ballad of Waterhole #3"

(Answers page 143)

SAME SONG—DIFFERENT SINGER

The following songs were a hit for two of the three singers listed under the title of the tune. Can you pick the right two?

1. "All the Time"
   (a) Jack Greene   (b) Mel Tillis   (c) Kitty Wells
2. "Cattle Call"
   (a) Buck Owens   (b) Eddy Arnold   (c) Slim Whitman
3. "Don't Let the Stars Get in Your Eyes"
   (a) Willie Nelson   (b) Red Foley   (c) Ray Price
4. "Golden Rocket"
   (a) Larry Gatlin   (b) Jim & Jesse   (c) Hank Snow
5. "Cold, Cold Heart"
   (a) Hank Williams   (b) Bobby Bare   (c) Jerry Lee Lewis
6. "Ruby, Don't Take Your Love to Town"
   (a) Johnny Cash   (b) Johnny Darrell   (c) Kenny Rogers
7. "Louisiana Man"
   (a) Bobbie Gentry   (b) Kitty Wells   (c) Connie Smith
8. "Before This Day Ends"
   (a) George Hamilton IV   (b) Moe Bandy   (c) Eddy Arnold
9. "By the Time I Get to Phoenix"
   (a) Glen Campbell   (b) Wanda Jackson   (c) Connie Cato
10. "Alone with You"
    (a) Roy Orbison   (b) Rose Maddox   (c) Faron Young

(*Answers page 143*)

HOW MANY, HOW MANY,
I WONDER HIDE AND HUNT

Each of the song titles below contains a number in it. Those numbers are hidden in the puzzle below. They run forward, backward, up, down, and diagonally in all directions. The important thing is that all the letters are in a straight line. Another hint: If you are looking for the number four, for example, find it someplace other than *four*teen. The same goes for another number that might contain another in it.

```
H T F L E W T N I N O T Y M I L L I O N
V E O N W N A A T Y F Y U O R J I S S T
Y E T N Y U E G F O R T Y N I N E L I D
T N H O E N S Z A U N E D I V E P O N E
V O T H Y T S I O X Y N T N A F V A T H
N Y O Z Y E D F W D U I J A S F S D O F
D T R Y I E V V E X B N O W T U V E B I
O N W T D E R D N U H U D R O N E Z D F
P E X O S N E E N E R T I H T R I E N T
A W I X T O N E T H E O T U S I N D T Y
X T S A M E D R P O S V R E G R A Y F O
I D E X I T N H N Y W U I G S U Z T I N
T O Z I N E E T D R E T I F L L I R F E
E N E E T E N I N L A S Y T O U V O X R
N W O S U S M E T L F I F T E E N F Y L
I V M I I T H R N I L L O N R P U S O N
N E V X L S D E R D N U H E V I F L T I
D R T B O L V E V E N S O U H T H U O F
U Y S U T E U N I O N Z E N L L F T V I
V Z O N S H A V E X O N E E T X I S E F
```

1. "Just _____ More Time"
2. "Just Between the _____ of Us"
3. "_____ Steps to a Phone"
4. "_____ in the Morning"
5. "_____ Lonely Days"
6. "Give Me _____ Acres"
7. "_____ Little Johnson Girls"
8. "_____ Tons"
9. "_____ White Horses"
10. "A _____ Years or So"
11. "One _____ Children"
12. "Engine, Engine ⚹ _____"
13. "_____ Years Ago"
14. "8 × _____"
15. "A _____ Pair of Boots"
16. "A _____ Miles Ago"
17. "14 _____ Franklin Park Circle Hero"
18. "When I'm _____"
19. "_____ Miles Away From Home"
20. "Class of _____"
21. "Forty-nine, _____"
22. "Joe and Mable's _____ St. Bar and Grill"
23. "July 12, _____ 39"
24. "Looking for More in _____"
25. "_____ Miles an Hour"

(*Answers pages 144–45*)

HOW'S THIS FOR OPENERS?—PART TWO

Again, name the titles of the classic songs from which these opening lines have been taken.

1. "Who did you say it was, brother?"
2. "How many arms have held you"
3. "Hands that are strong but wrinkled"
4. "Some people say a man is made out of mud"
5. "Drinking beer in a cabaret"
6. "I hear a train a'comin', it's rollin' round the bend"
7. "How many times have you heard someone say"
8. "Well, hello there"
9. "When I was young, I had lots of pep"
10. "All day I've faced the barren waste"
11. "The big eight-wheeler rollin' down the track"
12. "The old home town looks the same as I step down from the train"
13. "From the great Atlantic Ocean to the wide Pacific shore"
14. "Far across the deep blue waters lives an old German daughter"
15. "Just because I asked a friend about her"

(*Answers page 146*)

WINE, WINE, WINE

This quiz tests you on the subject of wine songs, a derivative of the immensely popular drinking song. Match the singers with the wine songs they recorded.

1. "Tears Will Be a Chaser for Your Wine"   A. Loretta Lynn
2. "In the Shadow of the Wine"   B. Mel Tillis
3. "Warm Red Wine"   C. Robert Mitchum
4. "Who'll Buy the Wine"   D. Wanda Jackson
5. "Warmth of the Wine"   E. David Houston
6. "Gone With the Wine"   F. Charlie Walker
7. "Wine"   G. Ernest Tubb
8. "Wine, Woman and Song"   H. Johnny Bush
9. "Wonder of the Wine"   I. Ray Pillow
10. "Little Old Wine Drinker Me"   J. Porter Wagoner

(*Answers page 146*)

GOING IN CIRCLES—PART THREE

Here we go again with another spiral puzzle. You know how it works by now. There are fourteen song titles within the spiral. The last word in the first one is the first word in the second title and so on ad nauseam. We've provided a little help along the way with the first, seventh, and last titles as well as the recording artists.

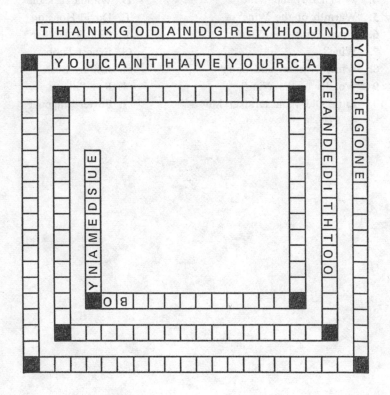

Roy Clark
Tompall and the Glaser Brothers
Porter Wagoner
Hank Williams
Delmore Brothers
Carl Perkins
Statler Brothers

Mel Tillis
Dave Dudley
Ray Pillow
Loretta Lynn
Carter Family
Johnny Darrell
Johnny Cash

(*Answers page 147*)

BIG

Can you complete the titles of the ten "big" songs listed below? The record-maker has been provided as additional help.

1. "Big _____"   Porter Wagoner
2. "Big _____ _____"   Jimmy Dean
3. "Big _____ _____ _____
   _____"   George Jones
4. "Big _____ _____ _____"   Lynn Anderson
5. "Big _____ _____"   Don Gibson
6. "Big _____ _____"   Buck Owens
7. "Big _____"   Marty Robbins
8. "Big _____ _____"   Dallas Frazier
9. "Big _____ _____ _____"   Johnny Dollar
10. "Big _____ _____ _____"   Buddy Alan

(*Answers page 148*)

77

HONKY-TONKIN'

Honky-tonk songs have maintained their enormous popularity since the early forties. Perhaps it is because we all have regrets and sorrows we'd like to lose or a reckless spirit we'd like to set free. Listed below are fifteen honky-tonk standards, spanning the past and present. Can you identify the singer forever linked with the song on record?

1. "Lovesick Blues"
2. "Flat Natural Born Good-Timin' Man"
3. "She Thinks I Still Care"
4. "Crazy Arms"
5. "Walking the Floor Over You"
6. "Bubbles in My Beer"
7. "Wild Side of Life"
8. "Crying Time"
9. "Don't Come Home A-Drinkin'"
10. "It Wasn't God Who Made Honky Tonk Angels"
11. "The Bottle Let Me Down"
12. "There Must Be More to Love Than This"
13. "If You've Got the Money, I've Got the Time"
14. "There Stands the Glass"
15. "Longhaired Redneck"

(*Answers page 148*)

COLORS

The task in this quiz is to remember titles with colors in them. As clues, the singer of the song and color in the title are provided. Every title made the country charts.

1. Green   Dottie West
2. Black   Leroy Van Dyke
3. Silver   Hagers
4. Pink   Carl Perkins
5. Yellow   Faron Young
6. Gold   Pee Wee King
7. White   George Jones
8. Brown   Billy Edd Wheeler
9. Blue   Loretta Lynn
10. Red   Roy Drusky

(*Answers page 149*)

PROGRESSIVE CRISSCROSS

This crisscross puzzle contains the names of well-known figures in the progressive country movement, sometimes known as "outlaws." One name should help you complete another. We've given you one name and supplied you with clues for the rest.

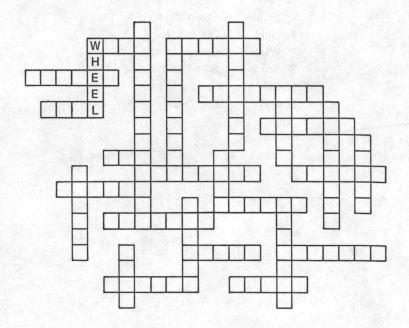

3 letters:
   "Longhaired Redneck"
4 letters:
   (first name) Daddy of a Revue
   "Groover's Paradise"
   "Sylvia's Mother" (last name)
   "Don't It Make You Wanna Dance"
5 letters:
   "Mr. Bojangles" (last name)
   "Help Me Make It Through the Night"
   "That Old Time Feeling"
   "Down in Mexico"
   "The Letter That Johnny Walker Read" (last word of group)
6 letters:
   "When I Get My Wings"
   "Mr. Bojangles" (second name)
   "Lost in the Ozone" (last name of group)
   "The Healing Hands of Time"
   "It's Morning and I Still Love You"
   "Put Another Log on the Fire"
7 letters:
   "Texas" (last name of band leader)
   "Door Number Three"
   "Red Neck Mother"
8 letters:
   "The Lady's Not for Sale"
   "This Time"
   "Sold American"
   "Heart Like a Wheel"
9 letters:
   "My Maria"
13 letters:
   "Me and Bobby McGee"

(*Answers page 150*)

AND THEN I WROTE . . .

Listed below are some of country music's most respected songwriters. Below their names are three well-known country compositions. Two of the three tunes are by the writer. Can you recognize the one that does not belong?

1. John D. Loudermilk
   (a) "Tobacco Road"   (b) "Still"   (c) "Waterloo"
2. Harlan Howard
   (a) "Candy Kisses"   (b) "Pick Me Up on Your Way Down"
   (c) "Heartaches by the Number"
3. Mickey Newbury
   (a) "The 33rd of August"   (b) "Love Is a Rose"   (c) "An American Trilogy"
4. Curley Putman
   (a) "Fraulein"   (b) "Green Green Grass of Home"   (c) "My Elusive Dreams"
5. Hank Cochran
   (a) "She's Got You"   (b) "Make the World Go Away"
   (c) "Secret Love"
6. Floyd Tillman
   (a) "I Saw the Light"   (b) "It Makes No Difference Now"
   (c) "Slipping Around"
7. Dallas Frazier
   (a) "The Son of Hickory Holler's Tramp"   (b) "There Goes My Everything"   (c) "Oney"
8. Ben Peters
   (a) "Before the Next Teardrop Falls"   (b) "Love Put a Song in My Heart"   (c) "Fire and Rain"
9. Don Wayne
   (a) "Country Bumpkin"   (b) "Saginaw, Michigan"   (c) "Easy Loving"

10. Shel Silverstein
    (a) "Skip a Rope"   (b) "One's on the Way"   (c) "A Boy Named Sue"
11. Boudleaux Bryant
    (a) "Bird Dog"   (b) "El Paso"   (c) "All I Have to Do Is Dream"
12. Ray Stevens
    (a) "Everything Is Beautiful"   (b) "Busted"   (c) "Mr. Businessman"
13. Scott Wiseman
    (a) "Too Late"   (b) "Mountain Dew"   (c) "Have I Told You Lately That I Love You"
14. Cindy Walker
    (a) "Bubbles in My Beer"   (b) "He'll Have to Go"   (c) "Warm Red Wine"
15. Guy Clark
    (a) "Texas—1947"   (b) "Like a Coat from the Cold"
    (c) "Wildfire"

(*Answers page 151*)

THE CANDIDATES

The political arena has attracted a number of country stars over the years. The following quiz asks you to name those who chose to run.

1. This country music great ran unsuccessfully for both the United States Senate and governor of Tennessee.
2. The author of the country classic "You Are My Sunshine" was governor of Louisiana for two terms, 1944–48 and 1960–64.
3. In 1952 a well-known singer-songwriter-movie actor chose to run for President on the Prohibition Party's ticket. Who was he?
4. This Opry superstar won the Republican primary for governor of Tennessee in 1948, but lost the final election.
5. One of the founders of the Light Crust Doughboys, this popular cowboy entertainer was elected governor of Texas while using the band to provide a musical background for his campaign.

(*Answers page 151*)

LEADER OF THE BAND—SECOND SET

Another matching quiz. Match the name of the band with the singer who fronts the band.

1. Jerry Jeff Walker	A. Tennessee Hat Band
2. Hank Williams	B. Bluegrass Boys
3. Del Reeves	C. Cowboy Twinkies
4. Faron Young	D. Golden West Cowboys
5. Hank Williams, Jr.	E. Second Fiddles
6. Bob Wills	F. Buckaroos
7. Rick Nelson	G. Lost Gonzo Band
8. Bill Monroe	H. Outlaw Band
9. Pee Wee King	I. Goodtime Charlies
10. Porter Wagoner	J. Drifting Cowboys
11. Tompall Glaser	K. Stone Canyon Band
12. Ray Wylie Hubbard	L. Country Deputies
13. Buck Owens	M. Cheatin' Hearts
14. Jean Shepard	N. Texas Playboys
15. David Allan Coe	O. Wagonmasters

(Answers page 151)

FRIED CHICKEN AND A COUNTRY TUNE

There are thirteen song titles needed to complete this puzzle. All the titles have something in common. To help you get started, the last names of all the recording artists have been scattered at random throughout the puzzle as well as the first and last letters of the songs.

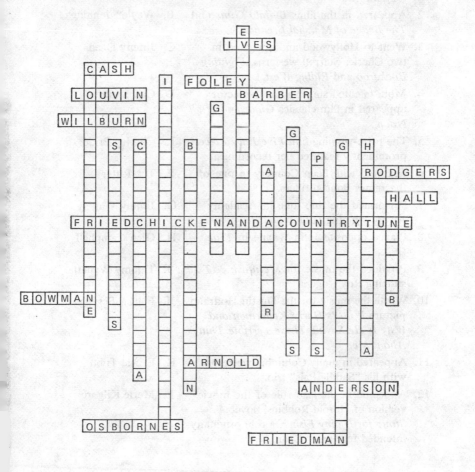

(*Answers page 152*)

SITTIN' IN THE BALCONY—SECOND REEL

Let's go back to the movies with a match-up quiz. Column one has the clues and column two lists the answers in scrambled order.

1. Performed the Academy Award-nominated song in *Sometimes a Great Notion.*

   A. Elvis Presley

2. Appeared in the films *Buffalo Guns* and *The Badge of Marshal Brennan.*

   B. Waylon Jennings

3. Went to Hollywood and appeared in two Charles Starrett westerns, *Fighting Buckaroo* and *Riding West.*

   C. Jimmy Dean

4. Multi-talented singer-comedian-actor appeared in film classics *Giant* and *High Noon.*

   D. Carl Smith

5. The prize-winning film *Five Easy Pieces* prominently featured her recordings.

   E. Charley Pride

6. Featured with Sean Connery in one of the James Bond thrillers.

   F. Tex Ritter

7. Performed the title tune in Academy Award-winning *High Noon.*

   G. Jimmy Wakely

8. Played opposite John Wayne in *True Grit.*

   H. Glen Campbell

9. Provided the music for *McIntosh & T.J.,* starring Roy Rogers.

   I. Tammy Wynette

10. Wrote the music for the Dustin Hoffman picture *Who Is Harry Kellerman and Why Is He Saying Those Terrible Things About Me?*

    J. Flatt & Scruggs

11. Appeared in many Columbia westerns with his "Saddle Pals" trio.

    K. Ernest Tubb

12. Appeared in the lead role of the movie version of Harold Robbins' novel *A Stone for Danny Fisher,* a role originally intended for James Dean.

    L. Merle Kilgore

13. Took acting jobs in several pictures including *Five Card Stud* and *Nevada Smith* for which he also provided the title song.

M. Rex Allen

14. Provided the exciting music behind the getaway scenes in *Bonnie and Clyde*.

N. Shel Silverstein

15. Has appeared in a score of films, but is probably best known for his work for Walt Disney, especially as a narrator.

O. Sheb Wooley

(*Answers page 153*)

HARD WORKERS

The working man. That's what America and country music are all about. Here are ten occupations and ten songs that extol them. Match the job to the song and the song to the artist.

1. Auctioneer	A. "Sixteen Tons"	a. Johnny Cash
2. Factory Worker	B. "Six Days on the Road"	b. Slim Whitman
3. Fisherman	C. "Wichita Lineman"	c. Leroy Van Dyke
4. Farmer	D. "Cattle Call"	d. Franklin Miller
5. Cowboy	E. "Blackland Farmer"	e. Glen Campbell
6. Mill Worker	F. "Muleskinner Blues"	f. Ernie Ford
7. Truck Driver	G. "Louisiana Man"	g. Fendermen
8. Railroad Worker	H. "Auctioneer"	h. Dixon Brothers
9. Coal Miner	I. "Oney"	i. Dave Dudley
10. Lineman	J. "Weave Room Blues"	j. Doug Kershaw

(*Answers page 153*)

PICK A PAIR—TWO

This is a two-part quiz. In each group below, two of the three artists scored a hit with the same song. Select the correct two out of three and name the hit.

1. (A) Everly Brothers (B) Flatt & Scruggs (C) Bobbie Gentry– Glen Campbell
   " _____ "

2. (A) T. Texas Tyler (B) Jimmy Dean (C) Roy Drusky
   " _____ "

3. (A) Red Foley (B) Roger Miller (C) George Morgan
   " _____ "

4. (A) Waylon Jennings (B) Wilburn Brothers (C) Don Gibson
   " _____ "

5. (A) Patsy Cline (B) Roy Acuff (C) Ray Price
   " _____ "

6. (A) Carlisles (B) Hagers (C) Hank Thompson
   " _____ "

7. (A) Jimmy Dickens (B) Charlie Rich (C) Charley Pride
   " _____ "

8. (A) Burl Ives (B) Billy Grammer (C) Bill Monroe
   " _____ "

9. (A) Jeannie Seeley (B) Willie Nelson (C) Mel Tillis
   " _____ "

10. (A) Claude Gray (B) George Jones (C) Tennessee Ernie Ford
    " _____ "

11. (A) Marty Robbins (B) Dick Curless (C) Lefty Frizzell
    " _____ "

12. (A) Connie Smith (B) Roy Clark (C) Johnny Cash
    " _____ "

13. (A) Hank Williams (B) Dave Dudley (C) Rick Nelson
    " _____ "

14. (A) Bobby Goldsboro   (B) Compton Brothers   (C) Ronnie Milsap
    "_____"

15. (A) Loretta Lynn   (B) Dottie West   (C) Jeannie C. Riley
    "_____"

(Answers page 154)

BROTHERLY LOVE

Find the answers to the following questions and write in the space provided. Then unscramble the circled letters to find one more famous brother act. Last names only, please.

1. This family introduced Loretta Lynn via their syndicated television show.
    __ __ __ __ __ (__) __

2. These brothers had a big pop hit in the sixties.
    __ __ (__) __ __ (__) __

3. These gents were known for their religious songs as well as their country hits.
    (__) __ __ __ __ __

4. These fellows are look-alikes.
    __ __ (__) __ __

5. These famous brothers are not known as a team.
    __ __ (__) __

6.
    (__) (__) (__) (__) (__) (__)

(Answers page 155)

WHAT'S IN A NAME?—PART TWO

Sometimes it takes more than talent to be a star. Match these well-known country personalities with their real names.

1. Jerry Reed	A. Virginia Hensley
2. Skeeter Davis	B. David Akeman
3. Rose Maddox	C. Leonard Slye
4. Minnie Pearl	D. Molly Beachboard
5. Roy Rogers	E. Marion Slaughter
6. Jimmie Driftwood	F. Mary Frances Penick
7. Patsy Cline	G. Jerry Hubbard
8. Vernon Dalhart	H. Rosea Arbana Brogdon
9. Molly Bee	I. James Morris
10. Stringbean	J. Sarah Ophelia Colley Cannon

(*Answers page 155*)

SCRAMBLER #5

Scrambled below are the names of four former Grammy winners.

1. SUDNOVAOTHID
2. LYRDMLJEOI
3. FHTODOAJRNRH
4. ENLEYAJIESENE

(*Answers page 155*)

ALL I HAVE TO DO IS DREAM

Like all writers, the country songwriter dreams and writes of dreams. Your job is simply to match the following dream songs with the artists who sang the dreams.

1. "Dreams of the Everyday Housewife"	A. Tex Ritter
2. "I Dreamed of Hillbilly Heaven"	B. Jimmy Newman
3. "My Elusive Dreams"	C. Carl Perkins
4. "Just Enough to Start Me Dreaming"	D. George Jones
5. "Until Dreams Come True"	E. Patsy Cline
6. "Country Boy's Dream"	F. Glen Campbell
7. "Daydreaming"	G. Jack Greene
8. "Send Me the Pillow You Dream On"	H. Johnny Tillotson
9. "Sweet Dreams"	I. Rusty Draper
10. "Something I Dreamed"	J. Jeannie Seeley

(Answers page 156)

GREETINGS

Fill in the missing word or words to complete these song titles.

1. "Hello _____"	Conway Twitty
2. "Goodbye _____"	Cowboy Copas
3. "Hello _____"	Orville Couch
4. "Goodbye _____"	Mel Tillis
5. "Hello _____"	Faron Young
6. "Goodbye _____"	Bobby Lord
7. "Hello _____"	Johnny Wright
8. "Hello _____ _____"	Wynn Stewart
9. "Hello, _____ _____ _____"	George Kent
10. "Goodbye _____, Goodbye _____"	Webb Pierce

(Answers page 156)

WHO WAS THAT LADY?

This is another Hunt and Hide puzzle. Hidden in the following jumble of letters are forty of the queens of country music. Look up, down, forward, backward, and diagonally in any direction and they're there. Here are a few clues to help you.

```
B E G Y A M O N T A N A U T A H L O U N
E T E R I E G W T W S C R C A L L E N U
A N N E R L R L E O Y K A A P E R T E Y
W I T L E O A I U N I R N R U D U A R S
Y V R L L Y F M R O S U N T H A R E O D
N A Y I T E W N P O M N A E J N M B R O
E D E M U G E N N D A L L R E O M A N S
T L L L B L L B U P A R S L G U P E I A
T I E L Y S N E T A H W S T R E E V K N
E H E P R A N D E R S O N R H V A J E U
K C S E J S G N W T D O A S T D N L R P
S R O M S K R E D O M Y I S Y A S N E O
H I B R I W S N E N C M V I W O A V S K
Y A T T E T B S R L T H O J N V A P H H
F F O E N A H O W A R D T A E N H S I R
R U S T Y E X G E V A I W C S I Y L S D
U J A E P A W B L O S U N K L Y L L E N
M V L H J Y R T U C K E R S E E R E J A
S I T S C O L T E R E L O O R O P W L E
R D H A L L E R D N A M J N Y E N I L C
```

1. A_____ _____ _____ _____ _____, Lynn

2. A_____ _____ _____ _____, Rosalie

3. B_____ _____, Mollie

4. B_____ _____ _____ _____, Pearl

5. C_____ _____ _____ _____ _____, Martha Lou

6. C_____ _____ _____ _____ _____, June

7. C_____ _____ _____ _____, Patsy

8. C_ _ _ _ _ _, Jessi
9. D_ _ _ _ _, Skeeter
10. E_ _ _ _ _, Dale
11. F_ _ _ _ _ _ _ _ _, Barbara
12. F_ _ _ _ _, Donna
13. G_ _ _ _ _, Crystal
14. G_ _ _ _ _ _, Bobby
15. H_ _ _, Connie
16. H_ _ _ _, Goldie
17. H_ _ _ _ _, Jan
18. J_ _ _ _ _ _ _, Wanda
19. J_ _ _ _, Norma
20. L_ _ _, Brenda
21. L_ _ _ _, Loretta
22. M_ _ _ _ _ _ _ _, Barbara
23. M_ _ _ _ _ _ _, Jody
24. M_ _ _ _ _ _ _, Patsy
25. M_ _ _ _ _ _ _ _ _ _, Melba
26. N_ _ _ _ _ _, Tracey
27. O_ _ _ _ _, Bonnie
28. P_ _ _ _ _ _, Dolly
29. P_ _ _ _ _ _, Jeanne
30. R_ _ _ _, Susan
31. R_ _ _ _ _, Jeannie
32. S_ _ _ _ _ _, Jeannie
33. S_ _ _ _ _ _ _, Jean
34. S_ _ _ _ _, Connie
35. T_ _ _ _ _, Diana
36. T_ _ _ _ _ _, Tanya
37. W_ _ _ _ _, Kitty
38. W_ _ _ _, Dottie
39. W_ _ _ _ _ _ _, Tammy

(Answers page 157)

93

BLUES CRISSCROSS

Blues and blue keep turning up in the titles of country songs. This crisscross challenges your recollection of those titles. As in preceding crisscrosses, one name should help you find another, thus crisscross. Fill in the blanks for the answers. We've started you off with Loretta Lynn's "Blue _____ _____."

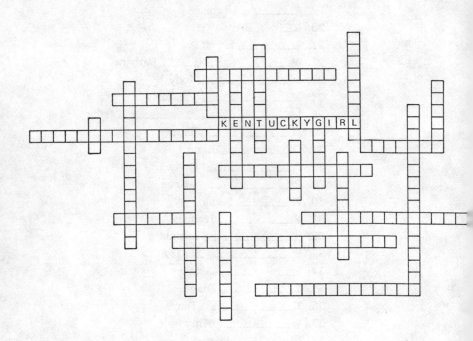

3 letters:
   "Blue _____," Jim Reeves
5 letters:
   "Blue _____ #4," Jimmie Rodgers
   "Blue _____," John D. Loudermilk
6 letters:
   "Blue _____," Sheb Wooley
   "Blue _____," Jimmy Newman
7 letters:
   "_____ _____ Blues," Bob Luman
   "Blue Eyes Crying in _____ _____," Willie Nelson
9 letters:
   "Blue _____ _____," Burl Ives
   "_____ _____ Blues," Marty Robbins
   "_____ _____ _____ Blues," Johnny Cash
   "Blue _____ _____," D. Statler
   "Blue _____," Ernest Tubb
10 letters:
   "Blue _____ _____," Carl Perkins
12 letters:
   "Blue _____ _____," Jimmy Newman
   "_____ _____ Blues," Johnny Cash
13 letters:
   "Bluebird _____ _____ _____ _____," Rose Maddox
14 letters:
   "Blue _____ _____ _____," Jim Reeves
   "Blues _____ _____ _____ _____," Delmore Bros.
16 letters:
   "I Cried the Blue _____ _____ _____ _____ _____,"
      Crystal Gayle
   "Bluebird _____ _____ _____," Tex Williams
   "_____ _____ _____ Blue," Hank Snow
19 letters:
   "_____ _____ _____ Blues," Lefty Frizzell

(*Answers page 158*)

COUNTRY ROCKERS

The quiz below again questions your memory on the rock 'n' roll backgrounds of some of country music's biggest stars.

1. No one would call this Country Music Entertainer of the Year anything but country, yet he performed as a member of the two classic rock bands, the Champs and the Beach Boys.

2. This *ole* country boy longed to rock like Elvis and Chuck Berry and even sold his first song to Sam the Sham and the Pharaohs before he found country stardom with "Baby Don't Get Hooked on Me."

3. He burst on the national scene as a replacement for Elvis with his No. 1 hit, "It's Only Make Believe," but who would have guessed he'd one day be recording massive country hits with Loretta Lynn?

4. From the day he recorded "Whole Lotta Shaking Goin' On," this country boy has been up and down and back and forth on both country and rock charts till it's best just to call him a purebred country rocker.

5. As leader of the rock group The First Edition, this popular performer found himself at the top of the rock charts with Mickey Newbury's "Just Dropped In to See What Condition My Condition Is In." This popularity continued through several popular rock albums, but the drift toward country became clear and distinct with his solo single on the country charts, "Love Lifted Me."

6. He became famous as one of TV's Monkees, but since their demise, he has distinguished himself with a critically acclaimed country trilogy.

7. A major rock force in the fifties and sixties, this country performer first recorded "Ooby Dooby," on the legendary Sun Label. This was followed by the platinum-record-winning "Only the Lonely" on Monument.

8. This talented performer burst on rock charts with "Ahab the Arab" and other novelty hits. He has remained both a country and rock hitmaker.

9. Two of his big rock hits were "I Wanna Love My Life Away" and "24 Hours from Tulsa." Later, he made the country charts singing with George Jones.

10. A preteen country virtuoso, he rose to fame as the leader of rock 'n' roll's "Sir Douglas Quintet." As a solo artist, he mixes the elements of both styles.

(*Answers page 159*)

REAL SPORTS

Name the country personality answering the following descriptions.

1. This country star sponsors a golf tournament that bears his name.
2. He gained his nickname by driving stock cars.
3. The leap from Super Bowl quarterback to country hit-maker was accomplished with ease by this Louisiana boy.
4. They called him the "Singing Fisherman" because of his love for the sport.
5. Sports car racing is a favorite diversion for the singer described as "Mr. Teardrop."
6. The ultraconservative "Day of Decision" was a hit for this rodeo-riding cowboy.
7. This country star's knowledge of golf earned him the job of color commentator on CBS-TV's tournament coverage.
8. A graduate of the honky-tonk, this artist gained his nickname as an excellent southpaw boxer.
9. Besides owning her own town, this superstar sponsors her own rodeo.
10. Because of this star's fondness for sports car racing, one of his many acquisitions in the sixties was a race track.

(*Answers page 159*)

THE NAME'S THE SAME CRISSCROSS

For each of the following crisscross answers, you need to conjure the names of two or more singers with the same last name. Then, hopefully, fill in that name at the appropriate place. Each answer intersects with another, providing a clue as to what goes in the adjoining space. Thus, everything crisscrosses. Go to it.

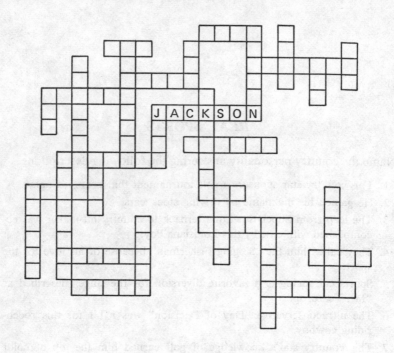

1. Mother, daughter, and Whispering Bill: (*8 letters*)
2. Ozzie's boy, the King of Austin, and an Earth Mother all share this name: (*6 letters*)
3. Try to keep up with these two Joneses: (*6 and 7 letters*)
4. We'll give you Sammi, you name the rest: (*3, 4, and 6 letters*)
5. They're not "Together Again," even though the name's the same: (*5 letters*)
6. One's all brass, one's often on TV, one hopes it's not the "End": (*5, 3, and 7 letters*)
7. Brenda was a rocker first and he was too: (*6 letters*)
8. She had a hit with "Quicksilver" and he was a star of *Frontier Doctor*. Last name, please: (*5 letters*)
9. One's a Delight and one's from *Hee Haw:* (*4 and 6 letters*)
10. Stonewall is one: (*7 letters*)
11. "Wolverton Mountain" and "Tennessee Waltz" royalty: (*4 letters*)
12. One lady is a best-selling Daughter and one is known for her western attire: (*7 and 4 letters*)
13. She was a Queen, he owns the King, and they share this name: (*6 letters*)
14. These Prices are right: (*3 and 5 letters*)
15. John wrote "July, You're a Woman," but who hit with "Love's Gonna Happen to Me"?: (*4 letters*)
16. He's never without his T, and she hit the fifties with "Bottle Me In": (*3 and 6 letters*)
17. Walkers Three: (*5, 5, and 7 letters*)
18. The late Hall of Famer and the "Girl on the Billboard" man: (*6 letters*)
19. Father and son Junior: (*8 letters*)

(*Answers pages 160–61*)

ODD BALL

In each group of unusual songs, select the one song that the singer did not record.

1. C. W. McCall
   (A) "Convoy"   (B) "Me and Ole C.B."   (C) "Wolfcreek Pass"
2. Don Bowman
   (A) "Chit Atkins Made Me a Star"   (B) "Wrong House"
   (C) "Understand Your Gal"
3. Jack Blanchard & Misty Morgan
   (A) "Tennessee Bird Walk"   (B) "Fire Hydrant #79"   (C) "Big Chief Buffalo Nickel"
4. Archie Campbell
   (A) "The Cockfight"   (B) "The Winner"   (C) "Rindercella"
5. Lonzo & Oscar
   (A) "You Blacked My Blue Eyes Too Often"   (B) "I'm My Own Grampa"   (C) "Waterloo"
6. Homer & Jethro
   (A) "Liberated Lady"   (B) "Battle of Kookamonga"
   (C) "Hernando's Hideaway"
7. Geezinslaw Brothers
   (A) "Chubby, Please Take Your Love to Town"   (B) "Charlie Brown"   (C) "Change of Wife"
8. Jimmy Dickens
   (A) "A-Sleepin' at the Foot of the Bed"   (B) "May the Bird of Paradise Fly Up Your Nose"   (C) "Chug-A-Lug"
9. Jerry Reed
   (A) "Alabama Wild Man"   (B) "When You're Hot, You're Hot"
   (C) "Sweet Thang"
10. The Carlisles
    (A) "Bed of Roses"   (B) "No Help Wanted"   (C) "Too Old to Cut the Mustard"

(Answers page 162)

IN THE JAILHOUSE NOW

The prison song remains one of country music's most popular forms.
Select the correct recording artists for the following prison songs.

1. "Life to Go"
   (a) Johnny Cash   (b) Merle Haggard   (c) Stonewall Jackson
2. "Jailhouse Rock"
   (a) Elvis Presley   (b) Bill Monroe   (c) Mickey Newbury
3. "The Prison Song"
   (a) Sonny James   (b) John Denver   (c) Roy Rogers
4. "Behind Those Walls of Gray"
   (a) Tom T. Hall   (b) Rusty Weir   (c) Roy Acuff
5. "Folsom Prison Blues"
   (a) B. W. Stevenson   (b) Johnny Cash   (c) Everly Bros.
6. "Sing Me Back Home Again"
   (a) Merle Haggard   (b) Moe Bandy   (c) Kris Kristofferson
7. "I Made the Prison Band"
   (a) Michael Parks   (b) Tommy Collins   (c) Tex Ritter
8. "The Wall"
   (a) Donnie Fritts   (b) Freddie Hart   (c) Billy Swan
9. "Ninety-Nine Years"
   (a) Bill Anderson   (b) Kenny Rogers   (c) Eddie Raven
10. "Christmas in Prison"
   (a) Gram Parsons   (b) Billy Cox   (c) John Prine

(*Answers page 162*)

THOSE TEXANS

In the following Hide and Hunt are hidden thirty country favorites born in the Lone Star State. Their names are concealed forward, backward, up and down or diagonally, always in a straight line. To help you through this wretched Texas mess here are the first names of all the people included in the puzzle.

```
A U T S T U C K E Y Y P I P T O S A E Z
S O L Y E L R E L L I M O S E P L O S E
T Y E J Y S T E A G A L L E A S L I N U
O I E O F R A S F R Y T S N W U I Y T G
I N T N L E N R U B A N T E R Y W U H I
M N A E G R I E F A A F L W V B U Y O R
E O I S R E D I Z V D R C B O E R T M D
L S D F D T O A E I R I L U N J E Y P O
O L M M O T L E L L A Z A R F O G R S R
N E A U W I Z T Y E D Z J Y O L T G O S
I N S M I R M S U A B E K L I E Y R N A
N H O M A N I C V C H L A R N N I E O H
G A T U B B A I A O K L W N E L B M A H
S L L E M H S M Z U R E Y P J S A A V U
S N R B L I S T U A L M R B E R Y Y U T
E D M A N D R E L L A I O G N E E R Y I
S G N I N N E J K U C I F A L L T A R P
G I L J O H T A M E M N I F I L R L T A
F O E Z B O W M A N A W L R O G E S U L
D R I L L W D O L L A R N E S O L S A T
```

1. Gene
2. Don B.
3. Mac
4. Jimmy D.
5. Dale
6. Kinky
7. Lefty
8. Claude G.
9. Stuart
10. Johnny H.
11. Waylon
12. George J.
13. Bob L.
14. Leon
15. Barbara M.
16. Roger M.
17. Willie
18. Mickey N.
19. Ray
20. Jim R.
21. Jeannie R.
22. Johnny R.
23. Red
24. Nat
25. Hank T.
26. Ernest
27. Tanya
28. Bob W.
29. Tex
30. Johnny D.

(*Answers page 163*)

I DIDN'T KNOW THAT . . .

There are some bits and pieces of information that will make your day a little brighter, as well as make you a riveting conversationalist at your next party.

1. She recorded "Baby It's Cold Outside" with Homer and Jethro.
2. Raising basset puppies is a favorite pastime for this singer-songwriter.
3. Operating an orphans' home is one of the many interests of this popular performer.
4. This Hall of Famer is credited with introducing the electric guitar to country music.
5. The Astrodome was the site of this star's marriage.
6. He was a member of Buddy Holly's famed Crickets.
7. A national furor was created when it was learned he had married a teenage cousin.
8. He went from a featured performer on the Opry to shoeshine man.
9. This superstar was a grandmother before her thirtieth birthday.
10. As a member of the Peace Corps, he introduced the Frisbee to Borneo.

(Answers page 164)

SCRAMBLER #6

Below are the scrambled names of four members of the Country Music Hall of Fame. One clue: they are all male.

1. HTKNTSACIE
2. RLBMENILOO
3. OYDRHGEAGE
4. PTSNLESEHHOSE

(Answers page 164)

WHAT'S 'ER NAME?

In this quiz, you are asked to fill in the missing word. Hint: Every missing word is a girl's name. In addition, the recording artists are listed, out of order, in column two. Your job is to put them in order and match them with the correct record.

1. "Tonight, _____"
2. "_____ (What's He Got That I Ain't Got)"
3. "I'm Not _____"
4. "Listen, _____"
5. "_____"
6. "_____ Was a Good Old Girl"
7. "Take a Letter, _____"
8. "Gettin' Back to _____"
9. "_____, You're Dreaming"
10. "Sweet _____ Jones"
11. "_____, You're Warm"
12. "Jack and _____"
13. "Take a Message to _____"
14. "Here Comes _____ Again"
15. "A Boy Named _____"

A. Kenny Rogers
B. Jim Ed Brown
C. Hank Cochran
D. Bob Luman
E. David Rogers
F. Sonny James
G. Leon Ashley
H. Waylon Jennings
I. Buck Owens
J. Johnny Cash
K. Everly Brothers
L. Marty Robbins
M. Jessi Colter
N. Dave Dudley
O. Anthony Armstrong-Jones

(*Answers page 165*)

FOOLIN' AROUND

There's always room for a sense of humor, as the following titles illustrate. Pick the artist who made a hit with each song.

1. "Junkfood Junkie"	A.	Statler Brothers
2. "Tupelo Mississippi Flash"	B.	Bobby Bare
3. "Just Blow in His Ear"	C.	Ray Stevens
4. "Ballad of J.C."	D.	Charlie Walker
5. "Cut Across Shorty"	E.	Johnny Cash
6. "Flowers on the Wall"	F.	Larry Groce
7. "Don't Squeeze My Sharmon"	G.	Jerry Reed
8. "Everybody Loves a Nut"	H.	David Wilkins
9. "The Streak"	I.	Nat Stuckey
10. "The Winner"	J.	Gordon Terry

(*Answers page 165*)

ANIMALS

Many songs have titles which include the name of animals. Insert the name of the correct animal and complete the following song titles.

1. "I've Got a _____ by the Tail"
2. "Never More Quote the _____"
3. "Sunshine and _____"
4. "Thank God and _____"
5. "Humphrey the _____"
6. "I'm Gonna Make Like a _____"
7. "Fried _____ and a Country Song"
8. "The _____ That Became President"
9. "Somebody Knows My _____"
10. "Six White _____"

(Answers page 165)

THE GROUP CRISSCROSS

Colorful and harmonious, the many groups in country music truly illustrate the diversity of its sound. Follow the rules as for all previous crisscross puzzles and enjoy yourself.

6 letters:

This California-based group soars on both country and rock charts.

8 letters:

Ozark-born modern country group featuring the bluegrass sound.

9 letters:

Pop was their patriarch.

11 letters:

Elvis' longtime back-up group.

12 letters:

"crik hoppers"

13 letters:

Dr. Humphrey Bates's band.

14 letters:

One of the first female country bands.
Featured mandolin pickin' of Frank Wakefield.
Regular on "WLS Barn Dance."
String band of Gid Tanner.

16 letters:

CMA Award-nominated progressive group.
Commander Cody's crew.
Pee Wee King was a member of this group.

17 letters:

Flatt and Scruggs and the _____.
Roy's cohorts, they now have a star on Hollywood Boulevard.

18 letters:

Same name as a long-running "country" TV series.

19 letters:

Famous radio group which spawned Bob Wills.
First country-rock group to tour Russia.

21 letters:

Headed by Charlie Poole.

22 letters:

Band organized by John Lair.

(*Answers page 166*)

ROCK 'N' ROLL INFLUENCES

The intermingling influences of country and rock over the years have made classifications of artists and songs academic. The following quiz illustrates the point.

1. This country performer was a member of the rock group Paul Revere and the Raiders and turned the Chuck Berry rock classic "Promised Land" into a country hit. Name the artist.
2. The original rock recording of "Blue Suede Shoes" was recorded by this influential country star.
3. As a member of the Byrds rock group, his influence led to their country-flavored albums. Later, he formed the country-rock group, The Flying Burrito Brothers.
4. Her early rock hits, such as "Sweet Nothins," while still a teenager catapulted her to fame. Now she is a regular hit-maker on the country charts.
5. Their early country hits, such as "Bird Dog" and "Bye Bye Love," put them at the top of the rock charts and made them regular guests on "American Bandstand."
6. In the fifties he was a rock 'n' roll teenage idol. Today he is a respected country artist with such records as "Country Fever" and "Bright Lights and Country Music."
7. He wrote the legendary Eddie Cochran rock 'n' roll hit, "Sitting in the Balcony," as well as Stonewall Jackson's historic country classic, "Waterloo."
8. Once a member of the rock group, The Uniques, he made the successful transition to country with such hits as "Soul Song" and "She's Helping Me Get Over Loving You."
9. By 1973 he was Country Music Entertainer of the Year, but rock 'n' rollers still remember his "Mohair Sam" and "Lonely Weekends."
10. A familiar name to rock fans in the mid-fifties, he scored big with "A Rose and a Baby Ruth."

(*Answers page 167*)

REMEMBERING HANK

The five song titles below all remember Hank Williams. Do you remember the stars who recorded the songs?

1. "Hank Williams, You Wrote My Life"
2. "Hank, It Will Never Be the Same Without You"
3. "Hank Williams Will Live Forever"
4. "Hank Williams' Guitar"
5. "Are You Sure Hank Done It This Way?"

(*Answers page 167*)

ANSWERS

SITTIN' IN THE BALCONY—FIRST REEL

1. Johnny Horton, *Sink the Bismarck!*
2. *The Big Country*
3. Molly Bee
4. Johnny Bond
5. June Carter Cash, *Gospel Road*
6. "Ode to Billie Joe"
7. Hank Williams, Jr., *Your Cheatin' Heart*
8. Conway Twitty
9. Jerry Reed, *W.W. and the Dixie Dancekings, Gator*
10. *Zachariah,* Doug Kershaw

STEP UP TO THE BAR

1. F		6. I	
2. H		7. D	
3. G		8. B	
4. E		9. A	
5. J		10. C	

SCRAMBLER #1

1. David Allan Coe
2. Freddy Fender
3. Merle Haggard
4. Johnny Rodriguez

HOW THEY GOT THERE

1. C	6. I
2. J	7. D
3. A	8. F
4. G	9. B
5. E	10. H

PURE GOLD

1. Johnny Cash
2. Eddy Arnold
3. Jim Reeves
4. Ray Price
5. Merle Haggard
6. Freddie Hart
7. Kris Kristofferson
8. Donna Fargo
9. Conway Twitty
10. Charley Pride
11. Lynn Anderson
12. Bobby Goldsboro
13. Jeannie C. Riley
14. John Denver
15. Mac Davis

EVERYBODY TALKS ABOUT

1. Cold
2. Tornado
3. Raindrop
4. Rains
5. Summer Skies
6. Sunshine
7. Snow
8. Rain
9. Wind
10. Raining

DEAR JOHN CRISSCROSS

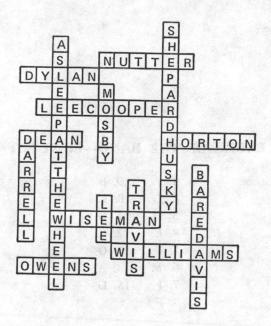

THE TROUBADOURS

1. H. Tom T. Hall
2. F. Johnny Cash
3. A. Roger Miller
4. I. Buck Owens
5. G. Merle Haggard
6. J. Kris Kristofferson
7. E. Loretta Lynn
8. C. Willie Nelson

9. D. Marty Robbins
10. B. Dolly Parton

g. "Faster Horses"
i. "Flesh and Blood"
h. "Kansas City Star"
e. "Crying Time"
f. "Branded Man"
c. "Loving Her Was Easier"
b. "Coal Miner's Daughter"
j. "Funny How Time Slips Away"
a. "Padre"
d. "We Used To"

LEADER OF THE BAND—FIRST SET

1. J
2. G
3. H
4. L
5. I
6. M
7. P
8. F
9. B
10. K
11. N
12. C
13. O
14. A
15. D

THE MEMORY LINGERS ON

1. "For the Good Times"
2. "Cold, Cold Heart"
3. "I Forgot More Than You'll Ever Know"
4. "(I'd Be) A Legend in My Time"
5. "Pick Me Up on Your Way Down"
6. "Faded Love"
7. "When My Blue Moon Turns to Gold Again"
8. "Half as Much"
9. "Lone Star Beer and Bob Wills' Music"
10. "Sweet Misery"

STABLEMATES

1. (B) U T T E R M I L K
2. R I N G E (Y) E
3. C H A (M) P I (O) N
4. K O K (O)
5. W H I (T) E   F L A S H
6. (T) (O) (M) (B) (O) (Y)

ODD ONE OUT

1. Connie Smith—Indiana (b)
2. Don Bowman—Texas (a)
3. Wynn Stewart—Missouri (c)
4. Buck Owens—Texas (b)
5. Red Steagall—Texas (c)
6. Dolly Parton—Tennessee (c)
7. Johnny Dollar—Texas (b)
8. Carl Belew—Oklahoma (c)
9. Webb Pierce—Louisiana (a)
10. Johnny Paycheck—Ohio (b)
11. Johnny Duncan—Texas (c)
12. Jean Shepard—Oklahoma (c)
13. Danny Davis—Massachusetts (a)
14. Buell Kazee—Kentucky (a)
15. Norma Jean—Oklahoma (c)

RADIO BARN DANCES

1. E		6. I	
2. J		7. C	
3. D		8. B	
4. F		9. A	
5. H		10. G	

1. Vassar Clements
2. Boots Randolph
3. Floyd Cramer
4. Charlie McCoy

GOING IN CIRCLES—PART ONE

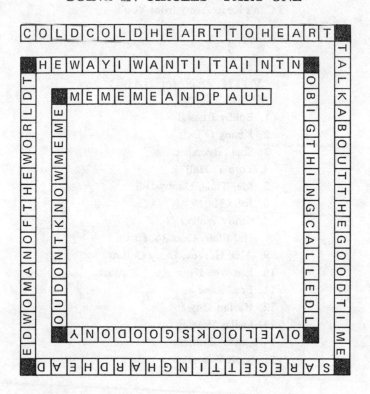

YOU CAN'T, I CAN'T

1. "You Can't Stop Me"
2. "I Can't Remember"
3. "You Can't Pick a Rose in December"
4. "I Can't Stop Lovin' You"
5. "You Can't Hurt Me Anymore"
6. "I Can't Be Myself"
7. "You Can't Have Your Kate & Edith Too"
8. "I Can't Get There From Here"
9. "You Can't Housebreak a Tomcat"
10. "I Can't Keep Away from You"

WITH PEN IN HAND

1. Bobby Russell
2. Kenny O'Dell
3. Shel Silverstein
4. Tom T. Hall
5. Mel Tillis, Danny Dill
6. John Hartford
7. Cindy Walker
8. Hal Blair, Don Robertson
9. Alex Harvey, Larry Collins
10. Pee Wee King, Redd Stewart
11. Fred Rose
12. Harlan Howard
13. Dallas Frazier
14. Curley Putman
15. Scott Wiseman

OUTLAWS

1. Willie Nelson
2. David Allan Coe
3. Billy Joe Shaver
4. Jessi Colter
5. Tompall Glaser
6. Jerry Jeff Walker
7. Sammi Smith
8. Waylon Jennings
9. Doug Sahm
10. Kris Kristofferson

I'M A TRUCK

1. B	6. B
2. A	7. C
3. D	8. A
4. C	9. C
5. D	10. D

SHOOTIN' STARS

1. B	6. A
2. C	7. H
3. I	8. J
4. E	9. D
5. F	10. G

NAME THAT STAR—PART ONE

OCCUPATION SONGS

1. F. Waitress
2. I. Trucker
3. E. Stripper
4. J. Carpenter
5. B. Salesman
6. A. Newsboy
7. C. D.J.
8. D. Hairdresser
9. G. Sailor
10. H. Sheriff

d. Stoney Edwards
a. Johnny Russell
f. Jim Ed Brown
h. Johnny Cash & June Carter
j. Jim & Jesse
i. Mac Wiseman
c. Stonewall Jackson
g. Kitty Wells
b. Hank Thompson
c. Rusty & Doug

HOW'S THIS FOR OPENERS?—PART ONE

1. "Just a Closer Walk with Thee"
2. "Crazy Arms"
3. "The Long Black Veil"
4. "He'll Have to Go"
5. "Me and Bobby McGee"
6. "Busted"
7. "San Antonio Rose"
8. "The Son of Hickory Holler's Tramp"
9. "Great Speckled Bird"
10. "Jambalaya"
11. "Louisiana Man"
12. "Dark as a Dungeon"
13. "Ode to Billie Joe"
14. "You Are My Sunshine"
15. "Ya'll Come"

THE EYES OF TEXAS ARE UPON YOU

1. "Long Long Texas Road"
2. "Yellow Rose of Texas"
3. "West Texas Woman"
4. "Texas—1947"
5. "T for Texas"
6. "Texas Plains"
7. "Beautiful Texas"
8. "Texas Rangers"
9. "Texas Morning"
10. "Texas Lullabye"

CHRISTMAS

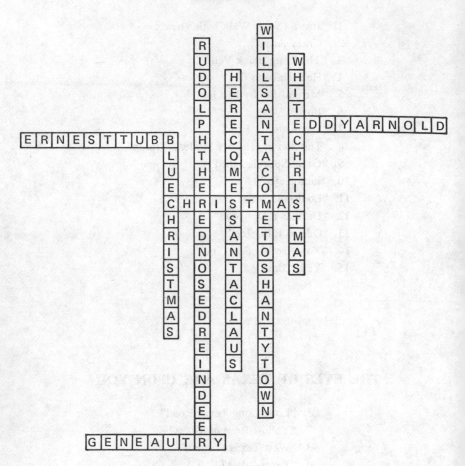

DOUBLE WHAMMIES

1.	F	14.	Y
2.	O	15.	D
3.	K	16.	S
4.	X	17.	W
5.	A	18.	U
6.	P	19.	I
7.	M	20.	H
8.	Q	21.	L
9.	B	22.	G
10.	V	23.	C
11.	R	24.	T
12.	J	25.	N
13.	E		

BEER DRINKING MUSIC

1.	D	6.	I
2.	E	7.	C
3.	G	8.	A
4.	H	9.	J
5.	B	10.	F

PARDON ME, MISS

1. c	9. a
2. c	10. b
3. b	11. c
4. a	12. c
5. b	13. a
6. c	14. a
7. a	15. b
8. b	

THE STATE OF THINGS

1. Kentucky	7. Arkansas
2. Kansas	8. California
3. Tennessee	9. Michigan
4. Oklahoma	10. Georgia
5. Mississippi	11. Alaska
6. Louisiana	12. Alabama

PIONEERS

1. D	6. J
2. F	7. B
3. A	8. E
4. I	9. G
5. H	10. C

GOING IN CIRCLES—PART TWO

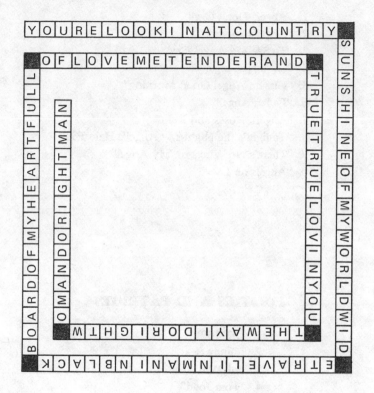

SCRAMBLER ※3

1. Ray Price
2. Sammi Smith
3. Lynn Anderson
4. Freddie Hart

HEAVENLY BODIES

1. "Angels Don't Cry"
2. "Angel's Sunday"
3. "To See My Angel Cry"
4. "She's No Angel"
5. "Kiss an Angel Good Morning"
6. "Fallen Angel"
7. "Angels, Roses and Rain"
8. "Tonight's the Night My Angel's Halo Fell"
9. "There's No Wings on My Angel"
10. "Angels on Leave"

POLITICS AND PATRIOTS

1. "PT-109"
2. Johnny Sea
3. Bob Wills
4. "Tom Joad"
5. "Franklin Roosevelt's Back Again"
6. Uncle Dave Macon
7. "The Americans"
8. Dixon Brothers
9. Aunt Molly Jackson
10. "You're Walking on the Fightin' Side of Me"

HOMESICK HIDE AND HUNT

```
A L L E Z Z I R P U G M A H I
K U O S R D G S S R E P O T N
M A L K V I N E L B M A H A L
G E R N I L O N T R P O P N Y
S R E G D O R O M A R D O Y N
L L V A H U S J R T O N I R N
J A N S O V K T O G I V R O N
S N E L T I O N R I S L N B O
O L D N E N O S I B O R L H
L O U D E R M I L K B P I L
T L S V I C T B U R U N Y S
K A H G O G D E T T E R L U D
I S A S H A V O M A T V K N I
L O L U N E V A K U N I L A R
Y A L L V U N P A I P G A H O
```

A THING ABOUT TRAINS

1. I   6. G
2. F   7. J
3. H   8. A
4. B   9. C
5. E   10. D

PRIME TIME

1. Glen Campbell
2. John Denver
3. Ray Stevens
4. Jimmy Dean
5. Burl Ives
6. Tennessee Ernie Ford
7. Red Foley
8. Mac Davis
9. Roger Miller
10. Lynn Anderson

WE MAKE BEAUTIFUL MUSIC TOGETHER

1.	D. Conway Twitty	f.	Loretta Lynn
2.	G. Waylon Jennings	j.	Jessi Colter
3.	J. Bill Anderson	b.	Jan Howard
4.	B. Don Gibson	c.	Dottie West
5.	A. Roy Drusky	d.	Priscilla Mitchell
6.	I. George Jones	a.	Melba Montgomery
7.	H. Buck Owens	i.	Rose Maddox
8.	F. Hank Williams, Jr.	e.	Lois Johnson
9.	E. David Houston	g.	Barbara Mandrell
10.	C. Jimmy Wakely	h.	Margaret Whiting

ALL OF ME

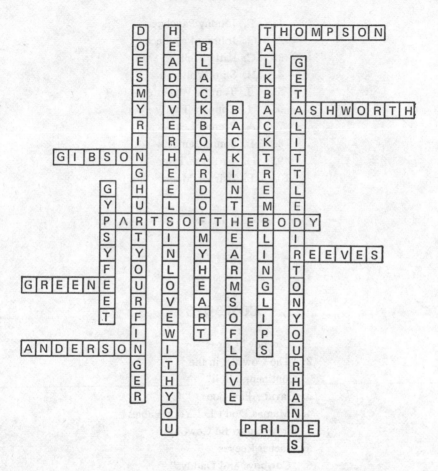

WHAT'S IN A NAME?—PART ONE

1.   E. Johnny Paycheck
2.   G. Johnny Paycheck
3.   C. Kitty Wells
4.   H. Slim Whitman
5.   J. Tammy Wynette
6.   I. Conway Twitty
7.   A. Brenda Lee
8.   B. Sonny James
9.   D. T. Texas Tyler
10. F. Warner Mack

COWBOYS

1. "Cowboy" Copas
2. "The Cowboy in the
   Continental Suit"
3. David Allan Coe
4. "Mamas Don't Let Your Babies
   Grow Up to Be Cowboys"
5. Goebel Reeves
6. "Cowboys and Daddys"
7. "Cosmic Cowboy"
8. Glen Campbell
9. "The Cowboy and the Lady"
10. "Honky-Tonk Stardust Cowboy"

INDIANS

1. "Kaw-Liga"
2. "Your Squaw Is on the Warpath"
3. *Bitter Tears/Ballads of the American Indian*
4. Marvin Rainwater
5. "Running Bear"
6. Ray Price
7. Billy Thundercloud and the Chieftones
8. Rcx Allen
9. "Geronimo's Cadillac"
10. Slim Whitman

COUNTRY IMPORTS

1. I A N and (S) Y (L) V I A (Canada)
2. (A) N N (E) M U (R) R A (Y) (Nova Scotia)
3. D I A N A (T) (R) A S K (Australia)
4. O L I V I A N (E) W (T) O N - J O H N (Welsh-born raised in Australia)
5. (H) (A) N K S N O W (Canada)
6. (A) (R) (T) (S) (A) (T) (H) (E) (R) (L) (E) (Y) (England)

WAY BACK WHEN

1. Kris Kristofferson
2. George Frayne (Commander Cody and His Lost Planet Airmen)
3. Johnny Cash
4. Guy Clark
5. James Talley
6. Shel Silverstein
7. Billy Joe Shaver
8. Eddy Arnold
9. Tammy Wynette
10. Jimmy Driftwood

MARY, MARY

1. "Sundown Mary"
2. "Mary Ann Regrets"
3. "Mary's Vineyard"
4. "Moods of Mary"
5. "Bringing Mary Home"
6. "Take a Message to Mary"
7. "Mary Don't You Weep"
8. "Mary Goes Round"
9. "Mary's Little Lamb"
10. "Hello Mary Lou"

TAKE ME OUT TO THE BALL GAME

1. Roy Acuff
2. Charley Pride
3. Gene Autry
4. Dave Dudley
5. Jim Reeves
6. Bill Anderson
7. Slim Whitman
8. Conway Twitty
9. Roy Drusky
10. Mayf Nutter

NEW DAYS, NEW WAYS

1.	J	6.	F
2.	G	7.	H
3.	E	8.	A
4.	B	9.	D
5.	I	10.	C

SCRAMBLER #4

1. Roy Clark
2. Glen Campbell
3. Loretta Lynn
4. Charlie Rich

PICK A PAIR—ONE

1. C	6. B
2. A	7. C
3. B	8. A
4. C	9. B
5. C	10. A

NAME THAT STAR—PART TWO

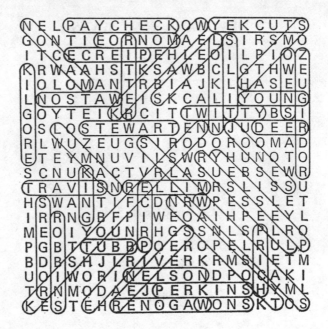

AN AMUSING CRISSCROSS

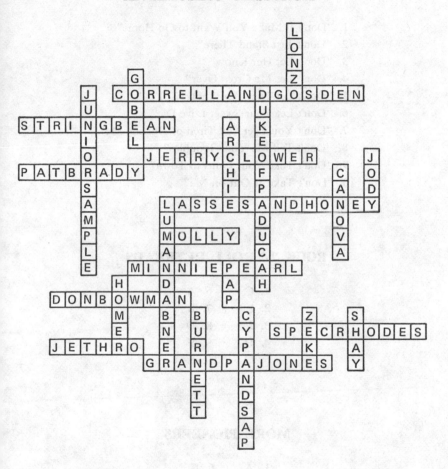

DON'T

1. "Don't It Make You Want to Go Home"
2. "Don't Just Stand There"
3. "Don't Let Her Know"
4. "Don't Let Me Cross Over"
5. "Don't Let That Doorknob Hit You"
6. "Don't Let Your Sweet Love Die"
7. "Don't You Ever Get Tired of Hurting Me"
8. "Don't Tell Me Your Troubles"
9. "Don't Take Your Guns to Town"
10. "Don't Take It Out on Me"

ROCK 'N' ROLL RETREADS

1. C	6. A
2. I	7. B
3. J	8. D
4. H	9. F
5. G	10. E

MORE PIONEERS

1. A	6. C
2. B	7. A
3. B	8. B
4. C	9. C
5. C	10. A

WAR SONGS

1. Johnny Horton
2. "Ten Thousand Drums"
3. "Smoke on the Water"
4. "The Soldier's Last Letter"
5. Jimmie Driftwood
6. "The Soldier's Sweetheart"
7. Dave Dudley
8. Roy Acuff
9. "There's a Star Spangled Banner Waving Somewhere"
10. "The Minute Men Are Turning in Their Graves"

NICKNAMES

1. H	9. A
2. O	10. C
3. J	11. E
4. L	12. N
5. M	13. I
6. B	14. G
7. K	15. F
8. D	

YOURS AND MINE

1. "Miller's Cave"
2. "Cattle Call"
3. "A Woman's Hand"
4. "Slowpoke"
5. "Louisiana Man"
6. "The Choking Kind"
7. "Cut Across Shorty"
8. "A Dear John Letter"
9. "All the Time"
10. "Raunchy"
11. "Alabam"
12. "Johnny One Time"
13. "Cold, Cold Heart"
14. "Don't Let the Stars
    Get in Your Eyes"
15. "Rocky Top"

THE DEVIL YOU SAY

1. DE(L) R(E)EVES
2. (W)AY(L)ON JENNI(N)GS
3. MARTY R(O)BBI(N)(S)
4. KR(I)S KRISTOFFERSO(N)
5. ME(L) STR(E)ET
6. (W) (I) (L) (L) (I) (E) (N) (E) (L) (S) (O) (N)
   ("The Devil in My Sleeping Bag")

HARD TIME HUNGRYS

1. Merle Haggard
2. "Busted"
3. "Coat of Many Colors"
4. "Hickory Holler's Tramp"
5. "Tobacco Road"
6. "Life's Little Ups and Downs"
7. Bobby Bare
8. "Peanut Butter Conspiracy"
9. Woody Guthrie
10. "Life Gits Tee-Jus, Don't It"

BALLADS OF . . .

1. D	6. G
2. I	7. A
3. E	8. B
4. F	9. C
5. H	10. J

SAME SONG—DIFFERENT SINGER

1. a & c	6. b & c
2. b & c	7. a & c
3. b & c	8. a & c
4. b & c	9. a & b
5. a & c	10. b & c

HOW MANY, HOW MANY,
I WONDER HIDE AND HUNT

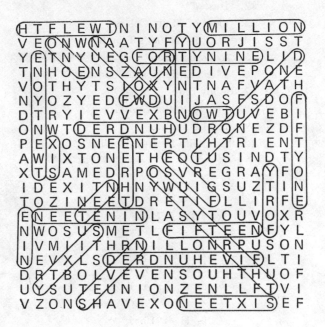

1. "Just *One* More Time"
2. "Just Between the *Two* of Us"
3. *"Three* Steps to a Phone"
4. *"Four* in the Morning"
5. *"Seven* Lonely Days"
6. "Give Me *Forty* Acres"
7. *"Five* Little Johnson Girls"
8. *"Sixteen* Tons"
9. *"Six* White Horses"
10. "A *Million* Years or So"

11. *"100* Children"
12. "Engine, Engine ⚹*9*" (Nine)
13. *"Fifteen* Years Ago"
14. "8×*10*" (Ten)
15. "A *Dozen* Pair of Boots"
16. "A *Thousand* Miles Ago"
17. 14*32* Franklin
Park Circle Hero"
18. "When I'm *Twenty-one*"
19. *"Five Hundred* Miles Away
From Home"
20. "Class of *Forty-nine*"
21. "Forty-nine, *Fifty-one*"
22. "Joe and Mable's *Twelfth*
Street Bar and Grill"
23. "July 12, *19* (Nineteen) 39"
24. "Looking for More in *Sixty-four*"
25. *"Ninety* Miles an Hour"

HOW'S THIS FOR OPENERS?—PART TWO

1. "Wreck on the Highway"
2. "I Really Don't Want to Know"
3. "My Woman, My Woman, My Wife"
4. "Sixteen Tons"
5. "Pistol Packin' Mama"
6. "Folsom Prison Blues"
7. "A Satisfied Mind"
8. "Funny How Time Slips Away"
9. "Too Old to Cut the Mustard"
10. "Cool Water"
11. "Movin' On"
12. "Green Green Grass of Home"
13. "Wabash Cannonball"
14. "Fraulein"
15. "She Thinks I Still Care"

WINE, WINE, WINE

1. D		6. I	
2. J		7. B	
3. G		8. A	
4. F		9. E	
5. H		10. C	

GOING IN CIRCLES—PART THREE

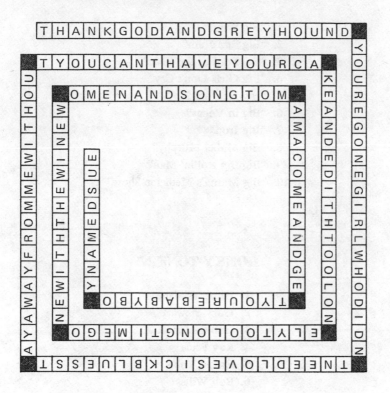

BIG

1. "Big Wind"
2. "Big Bad John"
3. "Big Fool of the Year"
4. "Big Girls Don't Cry"
5. "Big Hearted Me"
6. "Big in Vegas"
7. "Big Iron"
8. "Big Mabel Murphy"
9. "Big Big Rollin' Man"
10. "Big Mama's Medicine Show"

HONKY-TONKIN'

1. Hank Williams
2. Gary Stewart
3. George Jones
4. Ray Price
5. Ernest Tubb
6. Bob Wills
7. Hank Thompson
8. Buck Owens
9. Loretta Lynn
10. Kitty Wells
11. Merle Haggard
12. Jerry Lee Lewis
13. Lefty Frizzell
14. Webb Pierce
15. David Allan Coe

COLORS

1. "Before the Ring on Your Finger Turns Green"
2. "Black Cloud"
3. "Silver Wings"
4. "Pink Pedal Pushers"
5. "The Yellow Bandana"
6. "Silver and Gold"
7. "White Lightning"
8. "Ode to the Little Brown Shack Out Back"
9. "Blue Kentucky Girl"
10. "Red, Red Wine"

PROGRESSIVE CRISSCROSS

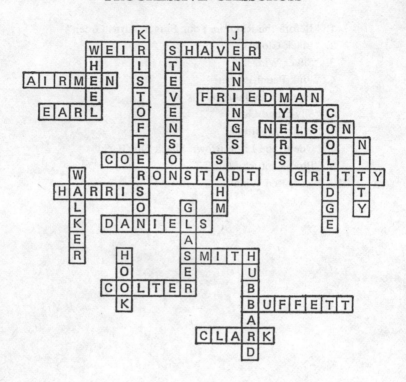

AND THEN I WROTE . . .

1. b	9. c
2. a	10. a
3. b	11. b
4. a	12. b
5. c	13. a
6. a	14. b
7. c	15. c
8. c	

THE CANDIDATES

1. Tex Ritter
2. Jimmie Davis
3. Stuart Hamblen
4. Roy Acuff
5. W. Lee O'Daniel

LEADER OF THE BAND—SECOND SET

1. G	9. D
2. J	10. O
3. I	11. H
4. L	12. C
5. M	13. F
6. N	14. E
7. K	15. A
8. B	

FRIED CHICKEN AND A COUNTRY TUNE

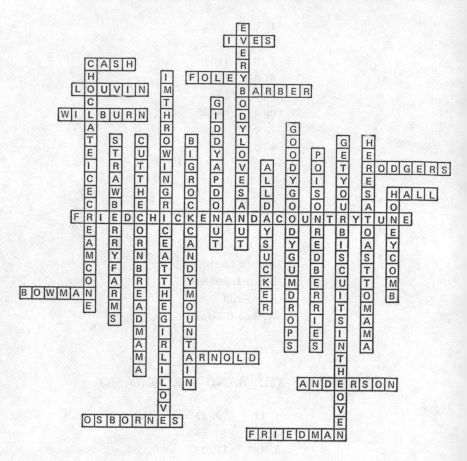

SITTIN' IN THE BALCONY—SECOND REEL

1. E		9. B	
2. D		10. N	
3. K		11. G	
4. O		12. A	
5. I		13. L	
6. C		14. J	
7. F		15. M	
8. H			

HARD WORKERS

1. H. "Auctioneer"   c. Leroy Van Dyke
2. I. "Oney"   a. Johnny Cash
3. G. "Louisiana Man"   j. Doug Kershaw
4. E. "Blackland Farmer"   d. Frankie Miller
5. D. "Cattle Call"   b. Slim Whitman
6. J. "Weave Room Blues"   h. Dixon Brothers
7. B. "Six Days on the Road"   i. Dave Dudley
8. F. "Muleskinner Blues"   g. Fendermen
9. A. "Sixteen Tons"   f. Ernie Ford
10. C. "Wichita Lineman"   e. Glen Campbell

PICK A PAIR—TWO

1. Everly Brothers, Bobbie Gentry–Glen Campbell
   "All I Have to Do Is Dream"
2. T. Texas Tyler, Jimmy Dean
   "Bumming Around"
3. Red Foley, George Morgan
   "Candy Kisses"
4. Wilburn Brothers, Don Gibson
   "Blue, Blue Day"
5. Patsy Cline, Ray Price
   "Crazy"
6. Carlisles, Hank Thompson
   "No Help Wanted"
7. Jimmy Dickens, Charlie Rich
   "Raggedy Ann"
8. Billy Grammer, Bill Monroe
   "Gotta Travel On"
9. Jeannie Seeley, Mel Tillis
   "All Right I'll Sign the Papers"
10. Claude Gray, George Jones
    "Family Bible"
11. Marty Robbins, Lefty Frizzell
    "Cigarettes and Coffee Blues"
12. Connie Smith, Johnny Cash
    "Cry, Cry, Cry"
13. Hank Williams, Rick Nelson
    "My Bucket's Got a Hole in It"
14. Bobby Goldsboro, Compton Brothers
    "Honey"
15. Dottie West, Jeannie C. Riley
    "Country Girl"

BROTHERLY LOVE

1. WILBU(R)N
2. ST(A)TL(E)R
3. (L)OUVIN
4. HA(G)ER
5. CA(S)H
6. (G) (L) (A) (S) (E) (R)

WHAT'S IN A NAME?—PART TWO

1. G		6. I	
2. F		7. A	
3. H		8. E	
4. J		9. D	
5. C		10. B	

SCRAMBLER #5

1. David Houston
2. Jody Miller
3. John Hartford
4. Jeannie Seeley

ALL I HAVE TO DO IS DREAM

1. F	6. C
2. A	7. B
3. I	8. H
4. J	9. E
5. G	10. D

GREETINGS

1. "Hello *Darlin'* "
2. "Goodbye *Kisses*"
3. "Hello *Trouble*"
4. "Goodbye *Wheeling*"
5. "Hello *Walls*"
6. "Goodbye *Jukebox*"
7. "Hello *Vietnam*"
8. "Hello *Little Rock*"
9. "Hello, *I'm a Jukebox*"
10. "Goodbye *City,* Goodbye *Girl*"

WHO WAS THAT LADY

BLUES CRISSCROSS

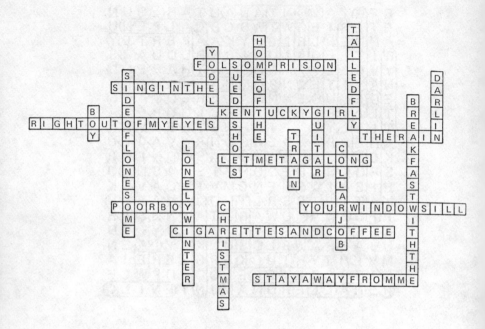

COUNTRY ROCKERS

1. Glen Campbell
2. Mac Davis
3. Conway Twitty
4. Jerry Lee Lewis
5. Kenny Rogers
6. Mike Nesmith
7. Roy Orbison
8. Ray Stevens
9. Gene Pitney
10. Doug Sahm

REAL SPORTS

1. Glen Campbell
2. Billy "Crash" Craddock
3. Terry Bradshaw
4. Johnny Horton
5. Marty Robbins
6. Johnny Sea
7. Charlie Walker
8. Lefty Frizzell
9. Loretta Lynn
10. Faron Young

THE NAME'S THE SAME CRISSCROSS

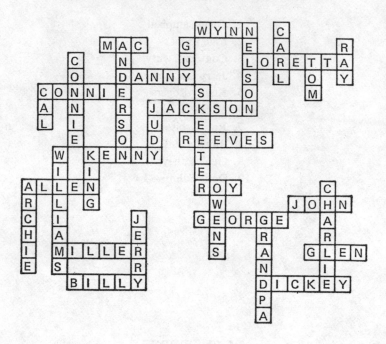

1. Anderson (Liz, Lynn, Bill)
2. Nelson (Rick, Willie, Tracey)
3. George, Grandpa
4. Sammi, Cal, Carl, Connie (Smith)
5. Owens (Buck, Bonnie)
6. Danny, Mac, Skeeter (Davis)
7. Dickey (Lee)
8. Allen (Rosalie, Rex)
9. Glen, Archie (Campbell)
10. Jackson (Wanda)
11. King (Claude, Pee Wee)
12. Loretta, Judy (Lynn)
13. Miller (Jody, Roger)
14. Ray, Kenny (Price)
15. John, Wynn (Stewart)
16. Tom (T.), Connie (Hall)
17. Jerry, Billy, Charlie (Walker)
18. Reeves (Jim, Del)

ODD BALL

1. B	6. A
2. C	7. B
3. C	8. C
4. B	9. C
5. C	10. A

IN THE JAILHOUSE NOW

1. c	6. a
2. a	7. b
3. a	8. b
4. c	9. a
5. b	10. c

THOSE TEXANS

```
A U T S T U C K E Y Y P I P T O S A E Z
S O L Y E L R E L L I M O S E P L O S E U
T Y E J Y S T E A G A L L E A S L I N U G
O I E O F R A S F R Y T S N W U I Y T G I
I N T N L E N R U B A N N E R Y W U H O R
M N A E G R I E F A A F L W V B U Y O R D
E O I S R E D I Z V D R C B O E R T M D O
L S D F D T O A E I R I L U N I E Y P O R
O L M M O T L E L L A Z A R F O G R S R S
N E A U W I Z T Y E D Z J Y O L T G O S
I N S M I R M S U A B E K L I E Y R N A
N H O M A N L C V C H L A R N N I E O H
G A T U B B A N A O K L W N E L B M A H
S L L E M H O M Z U R E Y P J S A A V U
S N R B L I S T U A L M R B E R Y Y U T
E D M A N D R E L L A I O G N E E R Y I
S G N I N N E J K U C F A L L T A R P
G I L J O H T A M E M N I F I R L T A
F O E Z B O W M A N A W L R O G E S U L
D R I L L W O O L L A R N E S O L S A T
```

I DIDN'T KNOW THAT . . .

1. June Carter
2. Tom T. Hall
3. Freddie Hart
4. Ernest Tubb
5. Doug Kershaw
6. Waylon Jennings
7. Jerry Lee Lewis
8. DeFord Bailey
9. Loretta Lynn
10. Kinky Friedman

SCRAMBLER ⚹6

1. Chet Atkins
2. Bill Monroe
3. George D. Hay
4. Stephen Sholes

WHAT'S 'ER NAME?

1.	L.	Carmen	9.	H.	Anita
2.	G.	Laura	10.	I.	Rosie
3.	M.	Lisa	11.	E.	Ruby
4.	N.	Betty	12.	B.	Jill
5.	A.	Lucille	13.	K.	Mary
6.	C.	Sally	14.	F.	Honey
7.	O.	Maria	15.	J.	Sue
8.	D.	Norma			

FOOLIN' AROUND

1. F	6. A
2. G	7. D
3. H	8. E
4. J	9. C
5. I	10. B

ANIMALS

1. Tiger	6. Snake
2. Raven	7. Chicken
3. Bluebirds	8. Monkey
4. Greyhound	9. Dog
5. Camel	10. Horses

THE GROUP CRISSCROSS

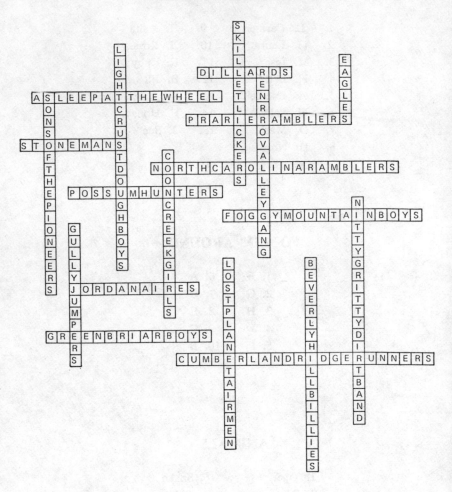

ROCK 'N' ROLL INFLUENCES

1. Freddy Weller
2. Carl Perkins
3. Gram Parsons
4. Brenda Lee
5. Everly Brothers
6. Rick Nelson
7. John D. Loudermilk
8. Joe Stampley
9. Charlie Rich
10. George Hamilton IV

REMEMBERING HANK

1. Moe Bandy
2. Ernest Tubb
3. Johnny and Jack
4. Freddy Hart
5. Waylon Jennings